PRAISE FOR
Sis, Take a Breath

If you're yearning for a real, honest conversation about how to handle the relentless stresses and demands of life, this book is for you. You'll immediately feel seen and understood, and as you walk through the pages of this book with Kirsten, you'll be changed. This highly practical book is what every woman needs to find the truest version of herself and live her most intentional life for Jesus!

KATY MCCOWN
Wife to retired NFL quarterback Luke McCown; mom of six; president of She Laughs Ministries; and author of *She Smiles without Fear: Proverbs 31 for Every Woman*

Sis, Take a Breath reads like a fun road trip with a friend—one you come out of as close as sisters with Kirsten, who has the gift of being straightforward and loving, honest and wise, vulnerable and strong. You will giggle, laugh, relate, learn, and come to love the journey even more after reading it yourself!

ELISABETH HASSELBECK
Emmy Award–winning cohost of *The View*; *New York Times* bestselling author

Like the older sister we've always wanted, Kirsten helps us feel understood and not alone with her conversational approach. She's intentional with her words and wisdom. This book will make you feel like you're sitting next to a best friend.

ESTHER FLEECE ALLEN
Bestselling author of *No More Faking Fine* and *Your New Name*

I absolutely love Kirsten Watson's energy and sweet spirit. It was a mystery to me how she kept both with seven kids at home and an abundant, busy life. Her amazing candor, humility, and wisdom shine in *Sis, Take a Breath*. A must-read!

REBEKAH LYONS
Bestselling author of *Rhythms of Renewal* and *You Are Free*

I'm in awe of Kirsten—she's not only a super mom, she's a superhero. In *Sis, Take a Breath*, Kirsten invites us into the grind, freeing us from the guilt. If you're isolated and overwhelmed, Kirsten finds strength in the struggle and shows us how you can too.

PAULA FARIS
Founder of CARRY Media; author; podcaster
Favorite roles: wife and mom

After spending time with Kirsten, I always leave feeling encouraged and challenged. *Sis, Take a Breath* is a fantastic extension of her heart as she teaches you how to walk with God and others in a genuine way.

COURTNEY DEFEO
Author of *In This House, We Will Giggle*

On these pages, Kirsten Watson has effectively married scriptural, spiritual truths with practical, honest applications. Her vulnerability and raw honesty invite the reader to know her, not as the pedestalized, beautiful NFL wife who has it all together and for whom life is perfect, but as a truly surrendered woman of God who is seeking to grow in Christlikeness in the midst of struggles common to all. As the road of life forks, we follow either the socially acceptable path of appearance management, settling for a life of *If it looks like everything is good, it must be and that's all that matters*, or the path of sanctification—the transforming process of becoming like Jesus, which requires honesty, vulnerability, humility, and community. Kirsten personally settles for nothing less than the road less traveled—the one that leads to growth in Christlikeness—and her heart desires that for each of us.

DR. VIRGINIA FRIESEN
Codirector of Home Improvement Ministries (HIMweb.org); coauthor of *The Marriage App*; author of *Raising a Trailblazer: Rite-of-Passage Trail Markers for Your Set-Apart Teens*

Sis, Take a Breath

Encouragement for the Woman Who's Trying to Live and Love Well

(but Secretly Just Wants to Take a Nap)

KIRSTEN WATSON

with Ami McConnell

TYNDALE
MOMENTUM®

A Tyndale nonfiction imprint

Visit Tyndale online at tyndale.com.

Visit Tyndale Momentum online at tyndalemomentum.com.

Tyndale, Tyndale's quill logo, *Tyndale Momentum*, and the Tyndale Momentum logo are registered trademarks of Tyndale House Ministries. Tyndale Momentum is a nonfiction imprint of Tyndale House Publishers, Carol Stream, Illinois.

Sis, Take a Breath: Encouragement for the Woman Who's Trying to Live and Love Well (but Secretly Just Wants to Take a Nap)

Designed by Julie Chen

Edited by Stephanie Rische

Published in association with the literary agency of Books & Such Literary Management, 52 Mission Circle, Suite 122, PMB 170, Santa Rosa, CA 95409

For information about special discounts for bulk purchases, please contact Tyndale House Publishers at csresponse@tyndale.com, or call 1-855-277-9400.

Library of Congress Cataloging-in-Publication Data

A catalog record for this book is available from the Library of Congress.

ISBN 978-1-4964-5680-9 (hc)

Printed in the United States of America

28	27	26	25	24	23	22
7	6	5	4	3	2	1

To my mom, who always taught me to take a breath
for myself and find what brings me peace.

To my people: Grace, Naomi, Isaiah, Judah, Eden, Asher,
and Levi. Thank you for giving me grace to do this book and
for all the "breathing practice" you've allowed me to have.

To my husband, Benjamin. You fought for my voice
to be heard even when I didn't think I had anything
to say. You are my biggest cheerleader. I love you,
and I'm so grateful God brought us together.

"Let everything that has breath
praise the Lord!"

(PSALM 150:6)

Contents

FOREWORD

Sis, take a breath. Breathing . . . that's effortless, right? Although the title of this book is a simple statement, it strikes a nerve with most women, giving us a unified call—and permission—to exhale!

We don't usually put much thought into how we breathe—that is, until we're instructed to do so. Breathing has been second nature for us ever since we entered the world as infants. As we continue living, a doctor might ask us to take a deep breath in order to listen to our lungs. We might also practice concentrated breathing during childbirth to help keep calm during the delivery process. During overwhelming experiences, we are encouraged to slow the pace of our breathing so panic doesn't overtake us.

My own journey of stopping to take a breath was often arduous. My twenty-six-year marriage to the guy some would say helped change the genre of gospel music (Kirk Franklin) began with a blended family when I was twenty-five years old. Our union thrust me into the spotlight and was accompanied by overwhelming expectations from others as well as from myself. My physical and emotional well-being were challenged as I made appearances on red carpets at the Grammys, Stellar Awards, and Dove Awards and as I juggled the demands of caring for my family and marriage. I distinctively remember the guilt I felt when my mind and body would signal that they needed rest, because, after all, I was supposed to have it all together—a false expectation I fed myself.

God has gifted women with so many talents, one of them being multitasking. But we often utilize this particular gift to our own detriment, feeding the unspoken pressure to be perfect. Unfortunately, social media has added to this dysfunctional thinking, perpetuating the need for women to present themselves as busy and put together at all times. It amplifies the phrase "She's a boss" when she just might be overwhelmed, falling apart, and internally dying. Although I've lived enough life to implement some healthier boundaries for myself, I, too, succumb to this tireless way of thinking at times.

This is why I'm so excited that Kirsten was obedient to God's call to share her heart of encouragement. We are all sisters in the quest to manage our commitments and prioritize our marriages, our children, and our careers. Most important, my sister, is the need to make sure we are placing ourselves as a priority on our own to-do lists. The Lord's command to rest is a great gift of love that we must surrender to.

Kirsten's unique authenticity and transparency will speak to young moms navigating the complexities of home, as well as to more seasoned women who need to be reminded it's never too late to begin. As you delve into the pages of Kirsten's heart through this book, I'm confident you will be encouraged to listen to your body, push past the guilt or pressure, and do what should come naturally: breathe.

Tammy Franklin

"HOW DOES SHE DO IT?"

"Seven kids and a pro-athlete husband. How do you do it?"

I get this question a lot. I still haven't gotten used to it. As the wife of Benjamin Watson, a sixteen-year veteran of the NFL, I'm comfortable walking down red carpets on my hot husband's arm as camera lights flash. I've given media interviews about what it's like for millions of football fans to learn I'm pregnant. But that's just a tiny sliver of my life. Maybe 2 percent.

What you don't see is the other 98 percent. The early

mornings when I'm up with bawling twin infants, sur-rounded by unpacked boxes from yet another cross-country move. Or the times when I've finally found a moment to myself and I hear a voice calling from the bathroom, "Mommy, can you come wipe me?" Or when I'm driving our twelve-passenger van across town for yet another flag football game. For the majority of my time, I'm serving my family behind the scenes, doing rather ordinary and unglamorous tasks.

So it's nice to be called out, to have someone imply that maybe I'm getting something right.

But when the question comes, it's also a little hard to answer. What kind of response could begin to make sense of my life? What sound bite could possibly cover that 98 percent? But perhaps the question is more important than the answer. What I know for sure is that this question comes from a place of deep hunger.

A hunger for insight.

A hunger for encouragement.

A hunger for understanding.

A hunger for truth.

I know because I'm asking it too. When I see some-one navigating the challenges and joys of womanhood and motherhood, I wonder, *How does she do it? What makes her tick? What keeps her going?*

I've always wanted a sister. Don't get me wrong—I love my brother, but there's a special bond that comes with sisterhood. Sisters are friends for better or for worse. When one grows, the others don't hold it against her. As things change, they don't judge. Sisters allow you to just be yourself and at the same time cheer you on to go further than you dreamed possible.

Whether you have a sister or not, I hope I can be that for you on these pages. I'm going to be vulnerable, open, and real—and encourage you to do the same.

I believe we're built for community. We're hardwired to learn from each other. In an increasingly disconnected world, we long to learn from each other's real-life stories. And while an Instagram story may look appealing on the outside, each of us secretly desires genuine connection, the knowledge that we're not alone.

So I've begun to honestly seek the answer to that question: How *do* I do it? As I share my story, I hope you will be able to find yourself on these pages too. Together we can walk this journey to loving and living well.

IN AN INCREASINGLY DISCONNECTED WORLD, WE LONG TO LEARN FROM EACH OTHER'S REAL-LIFE STORIES.

THE TRUTH ABOUT FAME

Let's start with one essential point: being married to an NFL athlete was never my plan. If anything, I was aiming for business success, not fame. Being famous for my relationship to Benjamin, or any man, never crossed my mind.

I met Benjamin when we were students at the University of Georgia. Like Benjamin, I was a college athlete. I was a softball player, and my teammates thought I should meet the new guy who'd transferred to UGA from Duke. Like me, he was a Christian. But I wasn't interested in dating a football player. Sure, I'd dated athletes when I was in high school, but I'd found that D1 college athletes were mostly next-level egos. I wasn't interested in any of that. Between classes and practice, I didn't have time for foolishness. I was ambitious and driven, and I knew my worth. My goal was to graduate with honors and have a corporate job waiting for me on the other side of that diploma.

> BEING MARRIED TO AN NFL ATHLETE WAS NEVER MY PLAN.

One activity I made time for was Fellowship of Christian Athletes (FCA) meetings. At one meeting the talk focused on godly dating relationships. I'll never forget when Benjamin raised his hand during the discussion. "My dad always told me that your relationship is like a triangle," he said. "You're on one corner and she's on the other, with God at the top. The only way to get close is to individually seek God." I remember thinking, *What's his name again?*

We got married after Benjamin's rookie year in the NFL. The average length of an NFL career is three to four years, so I figured Benjamin would play for five years, or maybe ten at most—because, after all, he's not average! If you'd told me that fifteen years later, we would have moved six times and had seven kids (including twins!) and I'd be a homeschooling, full-time mom, I would have laughed and assured you in no uncertain terms that you had the wrong girl.

Before Benjamin and I got married, we went through premarital counseling with our pastor. He asked how we imagined life once we had kids. Benjamin went first and calmly said he saw me staying home with our kids. My head turned so fast! I was working for Home Depot in California at the time. I had the clothes, the look, the expense account. I was like, "Wait! What? I have a career! I'm going to own my own company!"

Our pastor spoke directly to me, telling me I couldn't marry the "potential Benjamin"—the guy I hoped he'd be in the future. My *yes* would be to the man he was today and could potentially be for the rest of our lives. Could I commit to this man if he never changed? Thinking you can change another person is foolish. The only person I can control is myself—not anyone else.

I had been drawn to Benjamin because of his faith, his character, and his priorities. We shared those things on a deep level. In that moment, the Holy Spirit whispered to me, *You think you want to own your own company and you can hire a nanny to raise your kids. Whatever. Say yes to this man, and all will be well.* I did. I knew when the time came for us to have a family, we'd figure it out. Together.

BEHIND THE SCENES

Our first three years of marriage were hardly the "happily ever after" Disney promised. It turned out that marriage was hard work. Looking back, I realize that I was a piece of work. My husband was in the limelight, and I felt like I was competing for recognition. Everything about marriage felt so unfamiliar. We'd dated for years in college, but this was different. We were now living together and trying to do life with each other. Both of us are the oldest in our family, and we're super prideful, convinced we're always right.

That first year was especially tough. I remember one

argument in particular that produced a moment I'll never forget. Benjamin had these signings around the city where people stood in line to get their picture taken with him or get an autograph. Sometimes I'd join him at these events after work to get some time with him. One night I was sitting off to the side, irritated about our most recent tiff, when a woman came up to me.

"You're so lucky to be married to Ben!" she said. "He is so nice!"

I put on the best fake smile and replied, "He is nice."

Since we weren't speaking to each other, *nice* wasn't exactly the word I would have used to describe my husband at that moment. He was stubborn and disciplined and smart and so many things I didn't yet have the words to express. Yes, he was nice. But he sure could make me mad.

I loved Benjamin and wanted to be a good wife to him, but I was mostly trying to prove my worth. My focus was on me and what I could accomplish. This often resulted in butting heads with my new husband, who was working out his own stuff.

We'd been married about seven months when we realized we needed to seek some help. We loved each other; we just wanted to learn to like each other more. So we sought out some wise counsel from Paul and

Virginia Friesen, the couples' Bible study leaders for the Patriots, where Benjamin was playing at the time. (We've continued to do check-ins with them for more than fifteen years now.) We also went to a Christian marriage conference put on by an organization called Pro Athletes Outreach, and we liked it so much we've gone every year since. As we applied what we learned to the everyday moments of our marriage, our relationship became stronger. We now have the privilege of serving as directors of the event (called the Increase Conference).

By year three, we had put in the work—every day. During those years, God changed my heart in a lot of ways. Benjamin's and my love had grown, and now we were on the same page. We started discussing and praying about starting our family. We wanted to try for four kids.

Much to our joy, we got pregnant pretty quickly. We were giddy—it felt like we were sharing this wonderful secret. We were falling in love all over again.

We knew becoming parents would change us both forever, so we wanted to enjoy every moment before things took a radical shift. Together we planned a trip— a babymoon—and went out of the country.

The tiny island we stayed on was stunning. Our room overlooked the ocean, and the beach was beautiful. It would have been glorious . . . except I was so sick! The hormones from the pregnancy left me alternately ravenous and nauseated.

Benjamin knows how much I love to eat, so one night he made reservations at a romantic spot overlooking the ocean. We got all dressed up, and for once my nausea dissipated. Everything on the menu sounded good to me. The meal I ordered tasted great. Success! Then, as we headed back to our room, I broke into a run for the bathroom. Sure enough, I was sick again. *This is miserable,* I thought. *What a waste of money! We're in this enchanting place, and I'm spending all my time in the bathroom!*

As I lay on the floor, sick of being sick, the door opened. Quietly this six-foot-three, 250-pound man came in and lay down on the cold tile next to me. He didn't say anything; he just held me. In the middle of feeling so bad, I was enveloped in peace.

I'm not alone, I thought. *He's in this with me.* When I was at my weakest point, Benjamin valued me. I sensed the Holy Spirit saying to me, *Kirsten, you chose your man wisely.*

FAMOUS FOR WHAT?

Benjamin pretty much stayed under the radar for his first decade in the NFL. He made a lot of great plays and had a good reputation, but any notoriety he got was for the work he did in the community. As his wife, I'd pray for him to prosper. I prayed for the Lord to use us as a couple. I'd say, Lord, let him catch the winning touchdown. Or, Lord, let him find favor with this new team.

And Benjamin did prosper. He had an amazing sixteen years in the NFL (which is an exceptionally long career) with four teams: the New England Patriots, the Cleveland Browns, the New Orleans Saints, and the Baltimore Ravens. He was even nominated by the Saints and the Ravens for the Walter Payton Man of the Year Award. Still, he wasn't in the spotlight during most of his football career. National fame came into our lives in an unexpected way.

He wrote a Facebook post.

For as long as I've known Benjamin, he's been a writer and a deep thinker. One night we were at Target with our four kids, all four years and younger. We'd just left a community event and stopped to help a couple on the side of the road. After we helped them get a hotel room for a couple of nights, we stopped at Target to get a few items for them. I stayed in the car with the kids while Benjamin went inside.

The not-guilty verdict in the Ferguson case had been

announced the day before, which had us in a strange headspace. I'd seen Benjamin typing his thoughts on the notes app of his phone, but that was pretty typical. While Benjamin was in the store, VeggieTales kept the kids entertained in the car. Suddenly my phone started blowing up with texts from people who had seen Benjamin's Facebook post. This was a surprise to me because neither of us used social media much at the time. I thought Benjamin had pretty much forgotten it was even out there. His phone had powered off, so he had no clue that his post was going viral—shared almost half a million times—and was receiving national media attention. People appreciated the way he approached the topic of race with clarity and compassion and how he shared the gospel.

Suddenly everything in our world shifted.

I'd been praying that Benjamin's work in football would gain him a platform to share Jesus. With this viral post, I felt like God was saying, *Sit back, Kirsten. I've got this.* Benjamin's integrity and his extraordinary discipline on and off the field set the stage for him to share his faith in a totally unexpected way. God created a "for such a time as this" moment, ushering us into a new season as a family.

When I think of this, I'm reminded of Ephesians

3:20, which promises that God is able to do "immeasurably more" than all we ask or imagine. Isn't it strange how our most ambitious thoughts are tiny compared to God's?

SOMETHING TO SAY

When I worked as an intern at Chick-fil-A, I met my good friend Lauren. She invited me to join her at a Christian women's conference, where the speaker talked about lies the enemy uses against us. His goal? To keep us from the glory we're given in Christ to share with the world. Each of us has at least one lie that's specific to our story, and it typically comes to us when we're young.

I was happy to be at the conference, but the idea of having to discover and confront a lie I believed about myself didn't appeal to me. Still, not one to back down from hard things, I did the work of confronting my own lie that weekend. This turned out to be a game changer. Truly, it was a *life* changer.

When it's quiet, the lie I hear the enemy whisper to me is this: *You have nothing to say.*

Maybe you can relate.

Maybe the enemy whispers, *You're not special. What you feel doesn't matter. Your opinion is worthless.*

They're lies. Every one of them.

I'm ashamed to admit I believed this falsehood about myself. I knew my worth. I knew my intelligence. My parents raised me in the faith, with a strong moral compass. Discipline came naturally to me, and I had lots of ambition. Most of all, I was determined to live out my faith in a big way. Even so, speaking up was hard for me. Somehow I doubted the value of my own words.

So here I am, almost twenty years later. I've learned that the right words at the right time can be intense. Powerful. Life giving. As Scripture says, words have the power of life and death. Of course, some words are just noise. But words that are lovingly, respectfully shared about what we think, feel, and know? Words that are shared to speak truth and lift one another up? Words that are spoken to bring glory to God? Those words are worth sharing.

So yes, I have something to say. Something worth sharing. It starts with this: sister, take a breath.

I have a heart for my sisters who struggle, like I do, in the day-to-day. My deep desire is to invite you in to come and breathe with me.

My heart longs to speak to you. To encourage you, challenge you, and help you grow. I'm sharing from a place of love, truth, and realness. I won't take our time together for granted. Come as you are, with no judgment.

This isn't a how-to book; it's an act of sisterhood. I'll share "how I do life" as a starting place for our conversation. You'll probably laugh with me—and maybe cry a little too. Just know these two things: I will tell you the truth, and I won't shame you.

My hope is that, by the time you close this book, you'll feel emboldened and energized. And that you, too, will invite other sisters to breathe with you.

SISTERS

Every morning before my feet hit the ground, I whisper two prayers: "God, give me my manna for the day. Nothing more and nothing less. And Lord, all I have is five loaves and two fish. That's all I got. Please multiply them and let there be some left over. Amen."

In writing this book, I aim to share my experiences and insights about learning to breathe. I've homed in on topics that come up again and again in my intimate circle, on our podcast, and in my teaching ministry. I pray that as I share some life hacks and insights, you will be amazed at what God does with our loaves and fish.

Just a word about my use here of the word *sister*. I'm a believer and follower of Jesus Christ. That faith animates pretty much everything I do, so it's bound to come up in the chapters ahead. But whether you share that faith as my sister in Christ or are just curious about me and my life, please know that I welcome you into this space as a child of God, wherever you are.

There's a Latin phrase I love: *imago Dei*. It means "made in the image of God." You are *imago Dei*. You're God's own child, and you reflect His glory.

It's my privilege to share this journey with you, sister.

SISTERS ALLOW YOU TO

be yourself

AND CHEER YOU ON

TO GO FURTHER THAN YOU

DREAMED POSSIBLE.

CHAPTER 1

BREATHING LESSONS

Truth Talk

You shall know the truth, and the truth shall make you free.

JESUS

I'd finally made it back to the gym after baby number five. With all respect to all my sisters with ripped abs, I just don't enjoy working out. My favorite part of a workout is when I'm done. That salty pine smell and the clanging of metal weights invigorates some people, but me? The sight and smell of it at 5 a.m. had me wanting to crawl back in bed.

But Baby Eden was finally sleeping through the night, and getting out of the house felt like a small escape.

Maybe at the gym I could actually get something done. Maybe I'd sweat a little, log some miles, focus for a bit. Because in my day-to-day, with all the mouths to feed, diapers to change, laundry to wash, and schoolwork to oversee, I felt like my wheels were constantly spinning. That morning I wanted a win.

We'd recently moved to Baltimore for Benjamin to play with the Ravens. We still didn't know many people, so I'd gone online to find a gym and eventually booked time with a trainer. When I walked in, she greeted me with a smile and an outstretched hand. She was a tiny thing who appeared really strong—a look I was going for. This was starting off in the right direction.

My research had revealed that she had a PhD, so I figured she knew what I needed to do to get the baby weight off. The way she moved told me she was probably a dancer. I wondered if we'd be a good match.

After some weights and cardio, we finished the workout and she asked if I'd be open to incorporating some Pilates into our regimen. I was hesitant. I'd tried Pilates before and didn't like it—or maybe it didn't like me. So I asked why she thought this would be beneficial.

"Your core is weak," she told me. "Although you can do the movements, you're using the wrong muscles, and you aren't using your breath correctly."

Wait. What? Did I need to remind this PhD who I was?

She wasn't looking at a first-timer. I'd played high school and college athletics, I'd pushed out five babies, and I'd worked out my entire adult life. And did I mention I'd pushed out five babies?

My trainer pointed out that a good rule of thumb is that the body should exhale during exertion. "For example," she said, "on a pull-up, exhale while pulling the body toward the bar, then inhale on the way back down. Repeat."

Duh, I thought, I knew that . . .

As I held back an eye roll, I managed to laugh. "My breathing might be a little off, but I'm still here!" I said. "I must have been doing something right for the past thirty-six years, right?"

The truth was, I was insulted. I knew my body was a temple. I took good care of myself. And being married to a pro athlete, I'd spent countless hours preparing well-balanced, nutritious meals. As a mom, I cared for the health of my kids. And on top of that, there I was in the gym, with a weeks-old infant, putting forth my best effort. Didn't she know who she was dealing with?

BREATH IS BASIC

I'm so glad I held my tongue. Breath, I nearly said, is super basic. I've watched all my babies take their first breath. It's miraculous, sure, but it happens naturally, with no lessons. Nobody has to be taught how to breathe.

But then I started to wonder. Maybe she had a point. Exertion requires energy, and a deep hit of oxygen is probably needed most right after exertion. As a mom of a newborn, I thought it sounded pretty good to replenish my energy. By the end of that first grueling session with my trainer, I realized she was 100 percent right. Breathing might come naturally. But it isn't as simple as I'd thought.

> BREATHING MIGHT COME NATURALLY. BUT IT ISN'T AS SIMPLE AS WE THINK.

Back home, I started to notice my breathing throughout the day. I'd catch myself taking short breaths. Why was that? Short, shallow breaths might keep me alive, but they weren't sufficient for giving me the energy I needed. My body required real, deep breaths.

Sometimes I'd even notice I was *holding* my breath, especially in times of stress, like when my toddler bumped into something. I'd hold my breath, waiting to see whether he'd cry or carry on. Or when Benjamin got hit on the field. Or when I realized we'd be moving—again.

I was breathing. But I was depriving myself.

What my trainer had said was true, and until I accepted this truth, I'd be stuck.

BREATH IS LITERALLY THE STUFF OF LIFE. AND I'D BEEN NEGLECTING MINE.

I started repeating it throughout the day: *Exhale during the hard part; inhale to renew.* I said it when I was driving in traffic. When my kids argued. When my plans were interrupted.

That focus calmed me, restored me. It was nothing short of a breakthrough. As it turns out, breath is literally the stuff of life. And I'd been neglecting mine.

BREATH = TRUTH

Remember how God formed the first human being in the book of Genesis?

> The LORD God formed a man from the dust of the ground and breathed into his nostrils the breath of life, and the man became a living being.
>
> GENESIS 2:7

Did you catch that? God breathed *life* into Adam.

That same spirit—literally God's own breath—animates our lives. Without breath, we are just bags of bones and dust. Literally.

But something else happens in the next chapter of Genesis. Lies enter the world. Specifically, lies about God spoken by the "father of lies" (John 8:44).

Truth is a lot like breath. Jesus called himself "truth" in John 14:6: "I am the way, the truth, and the life" (NKJV). And when we read the Gospels, we find Jesus speaking the truth over and over again. Even when it was inconvenient. Even when it was unpopular. Even when it cost him greatly. Even when the cost of speaking truth was His own life.

In Jesus, there is no deceit. We might be deceived, but He never is. I want to be open to hearing and receiving the truth. I almost shut out the trainer when she was trying to share reality with me. I'm so glad I let it in. Our need for truth is as deep as our need for oxygen.

"YOU ASKED FOR IT, MOM"

Accepting truth is sometimes easier said than done.

Recently I asked my family to share some hard truths with me. As a parent, I correct my kids a lot. The Bible instructs me to do that—it's my job to train them and teach them. Their dad and I correct them because we love them. We regularly teach them that we aren't perfect, and we don't expect perfection; we simply want what's best for them, just as our Father in heaven wants what's best for us.

So the other day I sat down with the kids and asked each child to tell me one behavior of mine that's hard to deal with—something I can change or improve. At first they thought this was a joke. Or maybe a trick. Wouldn't they get in trouble if they offered something critical? I assured them this was an open invitation—a chance to *respectfully* speak the truth in love.

"Bring it on," I said. "You won't get in trouble. I really want to hear the truth."

Their responses were enlightening. The older girls wanted more quality time with me, while the other responses varied from not liking that I make them eat cereal for breakfast (I cook a full breakfast six days a week, so child, please. That ain't changing.) to my youngest feeling like I was mad at her when she called me to wipe her bottom in the bathroom. It was a good time of connecting for all of us. I left that conversation feeling known and loved—and committed to loving my people better.

Even if we've been living with a lie, we don't have to stay in that place. We can breathe through the hard part.

Exhale and inhale.

Is the truth easy? No. But I'll take an imperfectly said truth over a lie 100 percent of the time.

ULTIMATE TRUTH

Compassionate truth originates with God. To find and know truth, I spend time in the Word. Benjamin and I read a passage of Scripture on our own and then text our notes about it to each other daily. I try to do this before everyone gets up because otherwise life happens and people need me for . . . basically everything! Benjamin and I do Bible studies with the kids as well.

I honestly get so excited about digging into Scripture. It's something I look forward to—unlike going to the gym! The beautiful thing about it is, the more time I spend in God's Word, the more grounded I am in God's will for me. God's will is always good and perfect—and true.

I'm breathing that in—and breathing it in deep!

Your Turn to Take a Breath

Notice your breath right now. Try filling your lungs all the way to your lower belly. Hold it for four seconds, then release all the air till there's none left. Do this at least four times—maybe more, if you have time. How does it feel to focus on this simple, life-giving activity?

OUR NEED FOR TRUTH

is as deep as

OUR NEED FOR OXYGEN.

CHAPTER 2

I DON'T NEED EXTRA

Sticking with the Essentials

Self-care isn't saying no to everything,
it's saying yes to the right things.

RACHEL MORELAND

In an upscale café on a gorgeous fall day, I sat across from a TV producer and ten other ladies. We were all wives and girlfriends—sometimes referred to as WAGs—of NFL players who happened to be on the same team that season. I was looking forward to a meal where bibs and sippy cups weren't involved.

After the server took our lunch orders, the producer leaned across the table. "So, tell me," she said with a sly look. "What's the latest drama?"

"Drama?" I asked. "What do you mean?"

"You know," she replied. "Like, who do you have a beef with?"

I looked around the table. I knew these women. Several of us attended a weekly Bible study together. Most were moms. Between us, we were raising probably twenty-five kids. Some of us had careers outside of the home. All of us had our hands full, arranging busy school and sports schedules, feeding hungry bellies, navigating a relationship with a high-profile partner with a demanding career—all during the circus that is the NFL season.

"Try taking my kids to the grocery store," I said. "That's my drama!"

The table erupted in laughter. Someone explained to the producer that I held the title of "Mom with the most kids" on the team.

With the ice officially broken, one of the other ladies jumped in to share her personal beef du jour.

Imagine having to change your friend group practically every year. That's life in the NFL. Sometimes the personalities mesh well. Other times the clash is real. The gossip can get pretty toxic. Me? I don't have time for that kind of drama. In truth, who does? It's draining.

Soon our food arrived, and I dug in with gusto. As my people would tell you, I enjoy a good meal! I left lunch that day without picking up what that producer was laying down. I don't need extra (unless it's extra guac).

CLEANUP ON AISLE TWO

I was kidding about the drama at the grocery store.

Mostly.

When I take my kids shopping, I'm like a general going into battle. I have to gear up. Without leadership and discipline, I'm looking at destruction, injuries, possibly even mutiny. If you're a momma of young kids, you know what I'm talking about.

It starts with getting everybody in the vehicle. Can we talk car seats and boosters for a minute? The day I fasten my last car seat buckle will be a happy day! On the drive there, I tell the kids whose turn it is to ride in the cart and who stands on which side, holding on to the cart. I remind them to hold hands when we're walking in so we don't lose a kid. (Has this ever happened? Possibly!) Once we're at the store, I delegate, delegate, delegate. Busy kids are less likely to create a disturbance. Then I spout safety regulations: "Keep off the cart or it'll tip over." "Look where you're going or you'll run into someone."

And I manage disputes: "He ran over my toes on purpose!" "She was walking too slow."

And we haven't even gotten to their requests yet! That looks like me saying, "No. No. No. No. No. No. No." Peppered with the occasional "yes."

Even though we mostly stick to the perimeter of the store—produce, meat, dairy—those middle lanes are like a black hole sucking all my energy. "She picked the cereal last time!" "Can we try this, Mommy?"

There's so much *extra* at the grocery store.

WHAT'S EXTRA?

Here's what I mean by extra.

Bringing a snack to a class party seems like a pretty simple task. So when I got the request, I took a look in my pantry. I had a box of brownie mix, oil, and eggs on hand, so I said, "Sure." It would cost me a little time to put it all together, but I'm a team player, right?

Then I got an email telling me some kids in the class like this and don't like that—and since they're doing a unit on the Roman Empire, could the snack be something ancient Romans would eat?

Wait. What?

That's extra. It's over, above, and beyond. When something's over the top, that's extra.

When I agree to let the kids paint on the porch and, despite dressing them from head to toe in plastic and laying down tarps to catch the drips, somehow paint winds up on the couch upstairs, that's extra.

Extra can be

- behaviors (like drama or energy-sucking conversations)
- activities (like apps on a phone)
- even people

What's extra for me might not be extra for you, and vice versa. You may get a lot out of preparing cheese trays that ancient Romans would go wild for. Maybe that gives you energy and falls right in line with your priorities. For me, it's over the top.

The world tries to distract us with extra—that's for sure. It's a daily struggle, and it's not going anywhere. The older I get, the more easily I spot extra.

And the less I want it.

COUNT THE COST

An extra buck for guacamole is worth it, but the cost of "extra" can really add up. It can end up breaking the bank of your resources—and I'm not talking about finances, either. I'm talking about time and energy.

My friend Lysa TerKeurst is excellent at spotting

extra. Her book *The Best Yes* has been a game changer for many women of faith. Lysa realized one day that every "yes" she offers means less time, money, energy, etc. for herself and the people in her life. She had to figure out a way to make every yes worth the less. I'm getting better at this, but I have a long way to go.

My purpose in life is to bring glory to God. That's first for me, always. After that comes my commitment to my husband. My devotion to our children follows that. Then comes my larger circle of family and my friends.

When I add up those obligations and time commitments, I feel my head start to spin. I might even be tempted to crawl under the covers and sleep for the next two decades! Fortunately, a few years after that meeting with the TV producer, I got a wake-up call that changed my thinking about a lot of things. It was the beginning of "No-Extra Kirsten."

MIGRAINE WISDOM

Let me tell you about the time I came face-to-face with extra.

Benjamin had just signed with the Saints. I was happy for Benjamin, but it meant moving. Again. So we packed up the kids (four of them—which seems like

blessed! That phrase is one we all need to say now and again.

LIMITS ARE GOOD

Limits are a good thing. God made us in His image, but unlike God, we're not all-powerful. There are limits on human energy. For starters, there's just one of each of us. I am so outnumbered in our family, it's not even funny! I bet you feel that way some-times too.

> I'D LIKE TO KNOW WHO FIRST HAD THE COURAGE TO SAY, "I DON'T HAVE TIME FOR THAT." WHOEVER SHE IS, MAY SHE BE BLESSED!

Time is also a limit. God is not limited in time, yet He chose to give us just twenty-four hours in every day—and somehow we have to work some sleep in there somewhere. Thank God His mercies are new every morning.

Jesus brought the best, most radical news ever when He said that by saying yes to Him, we are children of the most high God. Because of Jesus and His death and resurrection, we are all God's children—male and female, people from every tribe, language, and nation.

When I know who I am—and whose I am—extra falls away like the dead petals on a flower.

God is in charge of the universe. All I'm in charge of is . . . myself. Of course I am responsible to the people I'm in relationship with: Benjamin, our kids, and then everyone else. But God is in charge of me. What a relief!

Knowing my true identity brings a healthy tension between humility and confidence. I'm not cocky, but I can face situations with courage because I know my place. Whatever situation I'm in (good or bad) is especially intended for me, and I know who ultimately has my back.

If it were up to me, I'd take on only what I can handle—actually, maybe less! In His sovereignty, God sometimes allows more than I can handle so that my relationship with Him is strengthened. It's part of how I become more the woman He created me to be.

When I choose wisely what I say yes to, it allows room for *His* extra.

PRIORITIES MATTER

Are you a fan of to-do lists? Sometimes I add an item to my list ("replace paper towels") just for the satisfaction of checking it off! (I know I'm not the only one!) Looking back at the previous week's to-do list is often a good indicator of how I've used my time.

What I do with today will shape the Kirsten I am tomorrow. This is pretty humbling stuff.

A while back, Benjamin and I decided we needed to prioritize time together. Our relationship is too important to take a backseat to extra. Now date nights are a priority, and we make time to get away as a couple on a consistent basis. After a lot of trial and error, we've learned that we have to dine early—even if it's uncool to have dinner at six. We still have to wake up early, no matter what time we get home!

Turns out I have to pivot sometimes—I have to reorient in ways large and small. So, date nights? Yes. Late nights out? Extra!

WHAT'S ESSENTIAL?

Over the course of sixteen years in the NFL, we moved five times. Each time, we packed up and moved to a new city where we knew very few people.

My body literally tenses up when I think about how it feels to arrive at a new house and see room after room filled with boxes. It's overwhelming.

So how do we tackle such a monumental task? We say, "What's essential?" If we arrived at night, we had to get the beds ready and the bathroom stuff unpacked so we could get good sleep. Everything else could wait.

That's how it is with extra. Determine what's essential, and then go from there.

My friend found herself in a season of being a single mom of young children. She had so much on her plate that she kept eliminating extra, like doing her hair (she cut it short), wearing makeup (fresh face!), and shaving her legs (pants, all the time!). A couple of years in, she realized she was taking better care of her kids than she was of herself. It wasn't sustainable. So she took stock and prioritized. She started gradually adding back in self-care.

"I talked to my kids about it and shared that I'd dropped the ball. I told them that things were going to change. They didn't know what to make of it at first, but it felt good to communicate my needs and let them know that I was being deliberate in the choices I made. Now I have more energy for everyone else, and I don't feel resentful because I'm taking better care of me."

When I say yes to anything extra, there's less room for extra in other areas of my life.

For example, Benjamin and I decided to take the kids on a Disney Cruise. We wanted to enjoy some intentional time together as a family, away from work and school. Of course, this meant extra on a lot of fronts in terms of preparation, planning, and expense.

When the week of the cruise finally arrived, our kids were amped. I was upstairs trying to pull things together for this big trip—for seven people—when all of a sudden I heard screaming. Somebody's tooth had gotten knocked out in a pillow fight. Working in that emergency trip to a dentist ate up all the margin I'd built into our days prior to the trip. I was so grateful I didn't have any other "extra" plugged into our schedule that week. Had I said yes to one other activity or invitation, we never would have made it to the ship—and I'm so glad we did, because we made some terrific memories together on that cruise.

Accidents happen, and when we look for it, we will always see grace. But could we do without extra? Yes. And if we're wise, we'll choose less extra.

SOMETIMES WE ARE SOMEBODY ELSE'S EXTRA

We have lots of personalities and needs to meet in our house. It can be a lot to make sure everyone's core needs are being met. For our family, we prioritize those needs into categories: physical, mental, and spiritual.

This is true for me, too, because if I'm not healthy, I can't be there for my kids.

When things get overwhelming, I can feel a rebelliousness in my spirit saying, *Wait! I didn't sign up for this.* That feeling is real, and it can drive *me* to do (or be) extra. So I've learned to pay attention to that warning sign.

God gave me free will for a reason. I may not be able to choose how I feel, but I get to choose what I do with those feelings.

I have a brain and a mouth. Wisdom is using my brain to evaluate and decide before my mouth gets invited to the party.

In all honesty, I'd prefer if people who love me would read my mind and give me what I want, when I want it. Is that too much to ask? Oh wait, it is!

Benjamin will tell you that the first few years we were married were tough. Looking back, I can see I was not an easy wife to deal with. We were both facing daily pressures, and I was very verbal about how I wanted him to prove his love for me. After all, God gave me a mouth for a reason, right? I used it to communicate my needs. A lot.

Poor Benjamin. Turns out I was being so extra!

My feelings and needs are important. But God never intended for Benjamin to handle them all. My family and my friends aren't meant to do that either. No human can. Only God can. He wants to be in communication with me. All. The. Time. And His shoulders are big enough to handle all my needs.

GRACE IS FOR REAL

Thank God for grace! When I'm weak, God provides grace. I repeat His words from 2 Corinthians 12:9 to myself all the time: "My grace is sufficient for you, for my power is made perfect in weakness." What a relief!

As your sister, I want you to hear this: no one is getting better when you're pretending to be what you're not. You don't need to be perfect. You don't have to be happy all the time. We're all made up of a lot of different emotions, and that's okay. You don't have to get everything right all the time. Be real with others. Be real with yourself.

God designed us to be real so we can grow. And breathe. Together.

Your Turn to Take a Breath

Think of a time when your mouth said yes but your heart was really saying no. How did that work out? How would you handle the situation differently next time? What extra do you need to cut out of your life?

GOD SOMETIMES ALLOWS

MORE THAN WE CAN

HANDLE SO OUR

relationship with Him

CAN BE STRENGTHENED.

CHAPTER 3

BITE YOUR TONGUE

Don't Say What You Don't Mean

I prefer to be true to myself, even at the hazard of incurring the ridicule
of others, rather than to be false, and incur my own abhorrence.

FREDERICK DOUGLASS

Benjamin was away at training camp, which meant I was home alone with the kids for about six weeks. And by alone, I mean *alone*, 24-7. During this time, when I was pregnant, with little ones running around, a new friend and I were talking on the phone. She had guests coming for dinner that night. She asked, "Kirsten, do you have a slow cooker?"

I laughed out loud because that question practically answers itself. I'm all for throwing a few ingredients into a pot in the morning and then, hours later, having the delicious aroma of roast, potatoes, carrots, and onions floating through the house. Is there anything more satisfying in the world? (Hard to believe that at one point one Crock-Pot could actually feed my entire family. Those days are long gone!)

So, short answer: yes, I have a Crock-Pot.

"Really?" she said. "Can I borrow it?"

"Sure. I guess I could drop it by . . ."

Now, let's press pause on this story for a minute. In my mind, I was being sweet. I was born and raised in the South, for goodness' sake! I figured she'd be sweet right back and say something like, "Kirsten, please! Don't be silly—you're pregnant with two little kids! I'll come by and pick it up."

Instead, she said, "Great! Can you have it here by lunchtime so I can get this roast started?"

Wait. What just happened?

In mere seconds, I'd gone from daydreaming about dinner making itself to committing to—let's be honest—an ordeal. If you've ever wrestled preschoolers (one of whom is potty training) into the car for an errand, you know what I'm talking about. That's to say nothing of the trip across town. And did I mention I was eight months pregnant? With a husband out of town?

I went from zero to straight-up irritated as I thought about what I'd stepped into. But at the same time, I knew full well this was my own fault. This situation was all on me. My friend hadn't even asked me for this favor! I'd *volunteered* to do this. Why? Because I wanted to seem sweet. I wanted the praise for being the nice friend.

Now how's a girl supposed to breathe when she's contorting herself like that? It's ridiculous.

This small-appliance fiasco turned out to be an eye-opener for me. Up until that point, I'd imagined that truth telling was for other people's benefit—that the moral imperative and scriptural command to speak the whole truth exists because lies hurt other people. What I was discovering was something bigger. Life is better when what comes out of my mouth isn't just accurate but also aligns with who I am.

> LIFE IS BETTER WHEN WHAT COMES OUT OF MY MOUTH ISN'T JUST ACCURATE BUT ALSO ALIGNS WITH WHO I AM.

HONESTY TAKES PRACTICE

Now if someone asks me to do something, I take a beat to really consider the implications. Here's my rule for myself: a yes from me is a wholehearted yes—I want to do it with my whole self.

When I take my own words seriously, it takes the pressure off. I can let my yes be yes and my no be no, as Jesus put it (see Matthew 5:37). It may be one word, but *no* is a complete sentence. *Yes* is too.

When I'm at war within myself, trying to talk myself into and out of things, it's such a waste of energy. This "I mean what I say" mentality helps me breathe.

A YES FROM ME IS A WHOLEHEARTED YES—I WANT TO DO IT WITH MY WHOLE SELF.

It's also really good for relationships. When people sense they have to guess what we really mean, trust is nearly impossible to achieve.

WHO AM I TRYING TO PLEASE?

In trying to get applause or props from my friend, I spoke quickly, without much thought. And that was only part of the problem.

I was trying to please others.

We learn early on that what we say has an immediate effect. Think of a baby whose momma either smiles or frowns based on the sounds that baby makes. Developmentally, children learn to make sounds that will produce the desired effect from their caregiver. It's a basic part of human communication.

The trouble comes when we let fear drive our

words—when we fear that our words will telegraph to someone that we're not nice. Not smart. Not independent. Not whatever. But when it comes down to it, does their opinion matter?

Listen, I was passionate in my pursuit of excellence in the corporate world. That didn't satisfy. I am passionate in my love for and commitment to Benjamin. But being his wife doesn't bring ultimate satisfaction. I love (and am driven up a wall by) my seven kids. But that won't satisfy either. What grounds me is the life and love of Jesus. My identity in Christ always satisfies. Knowing I am His beloved daughter clears the storm clouds in my mind.

SHE SAID/HE SAID

It's mind-boggling how we take for granted that people tell little white lies. And more than that, it's sad. Not to mention straight-up exhausting.

It takes vigilance to mean what you say all the time. But it's like a muscle that gets stronger with use. The more we do it, the easier it gets.

What we say to each other matters. Over the years I've joked to Benjamin that I sometimes wish a camera followed us around so we could get a "playback" of our arguments—to prove that I'm right! But humans don't come with recording devices. We don't always remember exactly what people say.

When Benjamin tells me he'll do something, he will do it. I trust him to back those words up with action because of his character. He won't break his word because he has a strong moral character and because he doesn't want to disappoint me. (Now *when* he'll do it . . . that's another conversation!)

WHAT A RELIEF!

If I agree to do something half-heartedly or if I verbally say something while thinking another, I'm being inauthentic.

Holding firm to my identity means I can be real with other people. I can say no without regret or shame. Because I know I'm saying yes to what matters.

Benjamin's father, Ken Watson, is an amazing preacher. I love to hear him speak whenever I get the chance. Once I heard him preach about the importance of keeping our word. He reminded us that we need to be careful about saying things we don't mean—and that includes the lyrics we sing. After hearing that, I started paying careful attention to the lyrics of praise and worship music. Candidly, I had to keep my mouth shut sometimes.

Several years ago, Benjamin and I went through the

painful experience of miscarrying babies—an experience I'll talk about more later in this book. For right now, let me just say that in the aftermath, my heart was so tender. It was really hard to sing along with some of the words of the praise songs: "Spirit, lead me where my trust is without borders" or "Thy will be done." My heart didn't align with those lyrics in that moment. So I let God know.

I said, "God, you know me. You know I'm in pain. I can't sing this with my whole heart yet. Heal this heart, Lord."

Y'all, He's trustworthy, and He can handle our grief. Practicing radical honesty—with God and myself—has really helped me heal.

"I'LL PRAY FOR YOU"

Praying for someone is a big deal. It means going before a holy God, petitioning Him on someone else's behalf. When I didn't have the strength to pray after my miscarriages, it was a gift to know that friends and family were praying for me. I could feel their prayers buoying me, keeping me from sinking into despair. When I've confided something to a friend and she's prayed for me, it brings me so much peace and comfort to hear from her in a text or phone call that lets me know she's going to the Father on my behalf. It makes me feel seen and loved. And known.

The opposite is also true: saying you're going to pray for someone and then not doing it is worse than saying nothing at all. It makes your words a lie. Those seemingly kind words, "I'll pray for you!" become a broken promise. There are other ways to show support, condolence, and love, so don't promise to pray unless you are serious about committing to that time and energy.

Imagine a huge medical bill came for you in the mail. It's an amount you absolutely cannot pay, so you're feeling really stressed about it. Shortly after you get the bill, you run into a friend who has a personal relationship with the CEO of the hospital you owe money to. When she learns of your predicament, she offers to speak to the CEO on your behalf to reduce the bill. You're so relieved! But while you wait, she does . . . nothing. Soon the hospital sues you for nonpayment. When you see your friend again, you ask her what happened.

She says, "I've been so busy, I forgot."

It would have been better for her to say nothing than to make an empty promise.

The same goes for us in prayer. Hold your tongue

instead of making an empty promise. Better yet, don't make the promise and then pray anyway! If you feel led to pray for your friend, stop right where you are and pray in their presence. Or make a reminder on your phone or on a Post-it. I have friends who devote certain days to intercessory prayer, so when they commit to pray, they have a designated time to make good on their promise. There are lots of ways to follow through—the point is, let your word be truth.

THE FREEDOM TO SAY YES

It's a privilege to be able to say yes or no. This freedom is precious. But make no mistake, it can be misused by those who lack consideration and decency. True freedom is not about doing whatever we want. It's not about simply being able to make a choice. Even animals can choose this or that option. Wisdom lies in choosing to spend our time, money, and effort for the best yes possible.

Not long ago I was invited to meet with the amazing women of MomLife Today, a community of Christian moms who support one another in the holy work of raising children. As these women told me about their vision, it spoke to something deep inside me. I wanted to say yes right away. But I held my tongue and took some time to think and pray about it, to seek the Father's wisdom and my family's support. Eventually the answer was clear: this would be a big yes for me!

MomLife Today has been such a blessing in my life. I get to interact with moms from all different perspectives who write and share articles to encourage one another, pointing us back to the One who loves us more than anything. That's what it's all about, really—turning our eyes to Jesus.

I love that we can share tips and tricks, but ultimately it's about the Word. Our motherhood must tap into and grow from that. After all, we can't give what we don't have. Serving as executive editor takes a lot of time and energy and resources, yet it also energizes me. I feel like I'm a part of something that helps other people—and something that feeds me, too. I'm glad I said yes.

EMPOWERED

Athletes love to quote Philippians 4:13. It's no wonder, since this truth is inspiring for anyone who needs strength, whether they're an athlete or a busy mom: "I can do all this through him who gives me strength." Break it down, and you see that the same God who created the entire world created little me—my toes, my hair, my brain, and my soul. And His power resides in me. That's a mindblower, honestly.

Anything I'm called to do, I can do through Christ.

"Through Christ" implies a dependency—an ongoing reliance—on the only One who is worthy of being relied on. Try reliance on anything else here, and you'll see how ridiculous it is.

"I can do all things through coffee that gives me strength." What? No way!

Or try these other substitutions:

- money
- status
- social media influence
- passion
- career

I'm not saying any of these are wrong; they're just not sufficient.

Putting all our eggs in any one of these baskets—depending on them to fulfill us—is foolish. I'm not trying to be Debbie Downer here; I'm being real. While this comes with a big dose of humility, it's also a source of hope. Humility, because we can't do this on our own. Hope, because Jesus is always sufficient.

Let's back up, though. Sometimes we get so excited about this powerful truth that we miss out on what comes right before it. Check it out:

> I know what it is to be in need, and I know
> what it is to have plenty. I have learned the
> secret of being content in any and every
> situation, whether well fed or hungry, whether
> living in plenty or in want.
>
> PHILIPPIANS 4:12

Did you catch that? Our *yes* to God can grow in confidence, even under the most challenging circumstances. When Paul wrote this letter, he was in prison. Drink that in for a minute. He was in chains—not free—yet he still gave thanks and praised God and encouraged the church. Talk about redeeming the time! He surrendered his life to God, over and over again, and as a result, he experienced God's peace and assurance. That wasn't something he earned; it was a fruit of his relationship with God.

Paul may not have been physically free, yet he had the freedom to choose how he would respond to his circumstances. He chose contentment, whether he was experiencing obvious blessings or significant challenges.

We, too, have the power to choose. May we have the wisdom to know when to say no so we can say a resounding yes to the things we've been called to. And may we choose contentment, no matter what's happening all around us.

Your Turn to Take a Breath

Truth takes practice. Make a commitment to speak only the truth today. If you mess up, it's okay—accept the grace freely given to you. Remember that God's mercies are new every morning (see Lamentations 3:22-23). At the end of the day, reflect on what it felt like to speak only the truth. What was challenging about it? What was freeing?

IT MAY BE ONE WORD,

BUT *NO* IS A

complete sentence.

YES IS TOO.

CHAPTER 4

WAGS

The Significance of a Significant Other

A good marriage isn't something you find;
it's something you make.

GARY THOMAS

Have you ever been to an NFL game? There's nothing quite like a full stadium on game day, buzzing with energy, enthusiasm, and hope. I still love to hear them call out my husband's name before the game starts—"Benjamin Watson!" After that, I'm done smiling. When someone you love is on the field, it's just as exciting, but there's also a lot to dread.

Our family gets to watch from the "friends and

family" section. The vibe there is a bit different from the rest of the stadium. It's more intense, thick with hyped energy, strong opinions, and frazzled nerves. Why? Because there's always a possibility that someone on the field will be injured. Think about it: these are serious athletes—and big guys. When somebody gets hurt out there, it's no joke.

Somehow over the years, the WAGs have gotten younger and younger, or maybe I'm just getting older (and wiser, I hope). Take, for instance, the smart young woman dating a former teammate of Benjamin's.

"Can I ask you a question, Kirsten?" she asked.

"Sure."

"How did you get Benjamin to propose?"

I laughed. *Get* him to propose?

Listen, sister. Forever is a long, long time. When you're signing up for forever, you want it to be with someone who is all in. You don't want to be stuck with someone who had to be strong-armed into getting down on one knee.

Think of it this way. My husband played for five different teams in the NFL. He poured blood, sweat, and tears into each game. Sure, there were highs, like winning the Super Bowl with the New England Patriots. There were also excruciating lows, like injuries that required surgery and months of grueling physical therapy. Each new contract Benjamin was offered meant we had to carefully weigh the options. The stakes were high. Would the benefits outweigh the costs? Would it be a win-win?

However appealing or risky, those contracts were for a finite amount of time. When it comes to sports, no contract is forever.

But when Benjamin asked me to marry him, he was offering a lifetime contract.

Forever. *For. Ever.*

I counted the costs. And I agreed.

It has taken us a lot of years to figure some things out. We put in the work—every day. We still do! Now I can say, without a doubt, that we are better together. I don't even want to imagine doing life without him.

But lure him? Girl, I'm not trying to trick anybody into forever. Single was working fine for me.

In my opinion, nobody's ready for the kind of partnership marriage requires until they can answer yes to the following:

Are you fine on your own?
Do you know your worth?
Do you know who made you?

You get to choose who you allow into your life. Don't just assume that because somebody wants you, you're gonna want them. You get to choose, so choose wisely. Whatever junk you bring to the marriage, he's not going to make it go away. And you can bet he's bringing his own junk too.

You are marrying the man he is now, not the man you know he could be. Marry the man he is today. That'll save you a lot of heartache!

RED PANTS AND A HOLY TRIANGLE

In the introduction I share about the first time I noticed Benjamin at an FCA meeting at the University of Georgia. He told the group about his vision for how marriage works—with partners growing closer to each other as they grow to know and serve God individually. That's what initially intrigued me about Benjamin. I felt instant respect and admiration for a man who firmly and proudly shared this wisdom and truth. It's what made him stand out in the crowd. Our friendship grew out of that first impression, and out of our friendship grew our romance.

Benjamin tells a different story. For him, our story actually begins before that FCA meeting. It was our sophomore year, and he had just transferred to UGA from Duke to play football. After the football team had finished training camp that summer, he went to a block party to see what campus life might look like. That's where he saw me, decked out in school colors—red, white, and black. That visual of me in red pants and a crisp white shirt made an impression, evidently. He jokes that a light shone down from heaven right in the middle of the quad. What's funny is that I don't remember seeing him then. Now did he talk to me? No. He just made a mental note. At the time we were both seeing other people anyway, so it really was for the best.

Later we became friends. When we were both single again, Benjamin took me out on what would be our first "date." I put that in quotation marks for a reason. He came and picked me up at my dorm, and we rode the campus bus—yes, the bus—to the school dining hall. Neither of us picked up the check because we were both on the campus meal plan! We joked about it then, and we laugh about it to this day. He told me, "Get whatever you want!" What mattered was that we were together, focused on each other. And that's how it is to this day.

REMEMBER YOUR STORY

When Benjamin and I tell the story of our romance, it strikes me that each of us comes at it from a different angle. We start at different places and recall different parts. Even though we were both there, we have unique perspectives. That's such a picture of how marriage works. I'm a very different person from Benjamin. As we say in our podcast, Benjamin is the "Why?" I'm more like, "Why not?"

In a very real way, sharing the story of how we met, fell in love, and made a commitment to each other matters. Research in neuroscience shows that revisiting memories and their accompanying emotions literally strengthens those connections.[1] We were designed this way on purpose. God made us to create memories together and to share our stories—for our sake and for the sake of those we love. I think that's why Scripture instructs us to remember God's good work, as in these words by King David: "Publish his glorious deeds among the nations. Tell everyone about the amazing things he does" (Psalm 96:3, NLT).

WHAT'S YOUR BLUEPRINT

Benjamin's triangle analogy made a big impression on me. It reflected our shared faith and values from the start. In fact, triangles were a big part of our wedding day. We arranged our candles in a triangle shape, we had triangles printed in the program—we even lit the Trinity candle (in a triangle shape) before the prayer. We wanted to illustrate that it's our deep desire to honor God first, above all else.

Jesus said, "Love the Lord your God with all your heart and with all your soul and with all your strength and with all you mind" (Luke 10:27). This priority comes first, always. When we make God our focus, we put all our relationships under His authority. What matters to God matters to us. Our significant other, our family, our friends, our neighbors—all these relationships are under the authority and will of God.

A lot of us get involved in romantic relationships with no real plan. Maybe the other person makes us feel good. Maybe we're attracted to his looks or money or reputation. All we know is we want to spend time with him. We're winging it. I'm not saying there's anything wrong with spontaneity, but when it comes to marriage—to forever, we need to be intentional. When we talk about permanent, we need to plan. If you want a house, you don't just start digging without a plan. That would be foolish.

Before Benjamin and I got married, we went through

premarital counseling with a pastor we respected. This was beneficial primarily because it guided our conversation. At our first meeting, the pastor said that if he felt we shouldn't get married, he would not marry us. We respected that—it helped us set our expectations.

Don't get me wrong, we still have plenty of issues. But the wisdom we received from our pastor helped us know what to anticipate in marriage. We were prompted to think through topics like finances, children, in-laws, holidays, and careers. Our counseling helped set the stage for situations we didn't know we would encounter. We became aware that even though we had differences, we had to agree on some nonnegotiables. Our foundation as a couple is in our belief in Jesus Christ. When you look at each other early on and say, "Not only do we agree to forever, but we have these nonnegotiables in place," it really sets you up for success.

I AM SECOND

Benjamin and I prioritize each other above every other living soul in this world. That's a big deal! When we examine the Word to discover what God wants for marriage, we find a wealth of wisdom. The apostle Paul instructs husbands to love their wives to the point of being willing to die for them, "just as Christ loved the church and gave himself up for the her" (Ephesians 5:25). Just let that sink in for a moment. Jesus didn't take a bullet for the church. He didn't step in front of a train. He was crucified on a cross! That's extreme torture. All day.

Since He was both fully human and fully God, Jesus could have easily gotten down from that cross. Did He? No. Because of His great love, He chose to die. That's serious stuff. It makes me glad not to be the husband, to tell you the truth!

Most translations of this passage in Ephesians instruct wives to "submit" as the church does to Christ. I don't disagree, but check out *The Message* paraphrase of Paul's instructions. It really fleshes out what Christ-like love looks like:

> Wives, understand and support your husbands in ways that show your support for Christ. The husband provides leadership to his wife the way Christ does to his church, not by domineering but by cherishing. So just as the church submits to Christ as he exercises such leadership, wives should likewise submit to their husbands.
>
> Husbands, go all out in your love for your wives, exactly as Christ did for the church—a love marked by giving, not getting. Christ's love

makes the church whole. His words evoke her
beauty. Everything he does and says is designed
to bring the best out of her, dressing her in
dazzling white silk, radiant with holiness. And
that is how husbands ought to love their wives.
They're really doing themselves a favor—since
they're already "one" in marriage.

EPHESIANS 5:22-28

Notice that this verse says a husband's leadership
comes by "cherishing." Not domineering, but cherishing. That's beautiful.

THE KIDS ARE NOT IN CHARGE

After God and my husband, my principal responsibility
is raising up my children in the faith. We're commanded
by God to bring up our children in the "discipline and
instruction of the Lord" (Ephesians 6:4, ESV). When
you have seven kids, that's a lot of discipline and a lot
of instruction!

You might think that with seven kids, they are the
center of our universe. And it's true that they take up a
lot of our energy, attention, and resources. But let's be
clear: our kids know that Mommy and Daddy prioritize
each other over everyone else, including them. We value

them. We love them. We teach them. But the hierarchy goes God, Daddy and Mommy, kids. Period.

In some homes, the kids are the focus. The parents may be paying the bills, but in fact, the kids are running the show. Sister, here's a truth bomb: making your children your highest priority isn't wise. It's not good for your relationship with your man. And it's not healthy for your kids.

God should be at the top of your priority list, and your spouse should come right after. When we do things in the divine order, the rest takes care of itself.

Remember, your children will only be in your house for a while. Lord willing, you'll be married for as long as you both live. Maybe you secretly think, *He can wait his turn to get attention. They're just kids; he's an adult. I'll have all the time in the world to pay attention to him when they don't need me as much.* Believe me, when you get around to him, it'll be too late. By then you won't have a relationship at all. If you nurture your relationship now, your children will thrive, knowing their parents' marriage is firm and secure.

ON THE SAME TEAM

When Benjamin and I are on the same team, we're a force.

When we were dating in college, we'd do game nights, boys versus girls. Benjamin would get hyped. And I mean hyped! He'd get in my face and be like, "Get ready to lose!" I'm just as competitive, if not more. So we would go at it. Those game nights were epic.

After game night, regardless of who won, we would be just a little irritated with each other for a few days. We were still speaking, but there was an underlying crack in the relationship. It wasn't like we were fighting; there was just tension that kept us from the closeness we desired.

I remember one time Benjamin showed up at my apartment with a homemade "I'm sorry" T-shirt. That's when we decided to put all our energy into rooting for *us* instead of pitting ourselves against each other. From then on, we made sure we were on the same team during game nights. And when that happens, everybody better watch out! We are fierce.

Together we are better. When our kids try to play us against each other, we just laugh. It never works. We are on the same team—we make sure of it. Even though we have different personalities and different responsibilities, we have the same goals. And we're rooting for each other.

Mark 10:7-8 says, "'For this reason a man will leave

his father and mother and be united to his wife, and the two will become one flesh.' So they are no longer two, but one flesh." Physically and spiritually we are one—we need to treat each other as we would treat ourselves.

Think about it: Would you hurt or injure yourself? Would you ignore something that was bugging you in your own body? In order for a marriage to flourish, we need to act like our husband's body is our body and his well-being is ours!

Being aligned like this is a spiritual practice as well as a physical one. I try to put in the work, knowing what we're building will only grow more valuable over time.

BETTER TOGETHER

With seven kids, I've done labor all the ways: in a hospital with pain meds, in a hospital without pain meds, at home with a midwife, in the operating room. All. The. Ways.

Baby number five was a home birth. By then Benjamin had been with me during childbirth enough to know the type of coaching I needed to get through it. See, I'm usually a talker. I love conversation, but active labor is *not* the time to talk to me. Breathing is extremely important, not only to get through a contraction but also to push out the baby.

I don't remember much about that delivery, but I distinctly remember Benjamin being outside the tub behind me, breathing with me. Instead of telling me to breathe, he inhaled and deeply exhaled *with* me. My brain was overloaded, so my rational functioning wasn't really working. I simply followed his breath, inhaling and exhaling, and that's how I delivered our baby girl.

Sometimes that's how it works for me in marriage. Benjamin and I talk a lot of things out. But sometimes I can just look at Benjamin. No words are spoken, yet we get energy from each other, knowing we're in this thing together. We will get through it, whatever it is. Good things come from this kind of together.

RESOLVING CONFLICT

I won't lie: I can get wrapped up in who's right or who's wrong. Actually, I'm generally right! There have been times I've spent an hour scrolling the internet to back up my argument with Benjamin. Ultimately, it's not usually that important who is right or wrong. God uses our conflict to show us things about ourselves that we're otherwise blind to, things he wants us to work through.

For me, it helps to try to get to the root of why I'm angry. For instance, Benjamin doesn't like to close drawers or cabinets. He is *able* to close drawers and cabinets, yet for some mysterious reason, he leaves them open. Early in our marriage, I would get upset because I thought he wasn't being sensitive. I was sure I could trace where he'd been by the open drawers he left in his wake.

> GOD CAN USE CONFLICT TO SHOW US THINGS ABOUT OURSELVES THAT WE'RE OTHERWISE BLIND TO.

One day I was feeling overwhelmed with all I had on my plate. I finally just sat down at the kitchen table and had a good cry. When Benjamin asked what was wrong, I said, "I'll be okay. I just realized I'm going to have to close drawers behind you forever." We laugh about that now. I knew he wasn't ever going to change that behavior (it annoys me to this day!), so I resolved to be honest about how it made me feel.

KEEP THE SPARK ALIVE

In all the houses we've lived in as a couple, we never had a non-gas fireplace. Until recently. I was so excited. It seemed so cozy and romantic to have a fire going in the fireplace while outside there was snow on the ground. So I had some wood delivered and got a fire started. It crackled and popped and smelled so good! I called Benjamin in to see what I'd done. He cheered along with me.

Then I left the room. I got busy and forgot all about the fire. The responsibility for keeping it going fell to him. He figured out how to keep those sparks from dying out. He stoked it, put some more wood on, and stoked it some more.

It takes intentional effort and prioritizing to keep a fire going. Otherwise it goes out. Sure, you can get it started again, but it's so much easier to maintain it than to begin from scratch.

A great way to keep the marriage fire going is to make it clear to yourself (and others) that your marriage is a priority. Date each other! When we started going out for date nights, just the two of us, our kids said, "You don't love us!"

> THE DEVIL LOSES WHEN YOUR MARRIAGE THRIVES, SO YOU CAN EXPECT HIM TO TRY TO KEEP Y'ALL APART.

I told them, "We are doing date night so we will be better parents." Our message to them before we leave is, "We love you. Bye!"

Your kids may act like they don't want you to go. Do it anyway. Now that we've established this habit, our kids expect it. They see that date night is good for the health of our marriage and our individual sanity. (It also helps to have a great babysitter!)

I'm such a foodie that we almost always do dinner out. I plan my outfit. I wear makeup and heels, and I even put on eyelashes just because I know Benjamin likes it. Make it something you really look forward to. Anticipating that time with each other makes it even more special!

The devil loses when your marriage thrives, so you can expect him to start trying to keep y'all apart. Don't be surprised to hear him whisper objections in your ear the moment you decide to do date night.

You don't have time.
Babysitters are too expensive.
There are so many other things that need to be done!
We don't even like the same things.
Who's gonna watch the kids?

Stick with it, despite the objections. You might have to get creative, but you can make it work for you. Your date might look radically different from ours, as it should. Each couple is unique.

Over the years, our date nights have changed as our life has changed. These days we have to be up at 6:30 a.m., so late nights are off the table. We do early dinners. I mean really early! Like eating with the old folks early. Since nobody else eats that early, we're always able to get reservations. When we get home, our kids are asleep and the kitchen is clean. It makes me smile just thinking of it.

Date nights are a taste of what it was like when it was just us, before kids. It will be that way again when they're all grown. Creating this intentional time together is a great reminder of who we are as a couple. Not the Watson Nine, just the Watson Duo.

Me and Benjamin. Forever.

ALL THE SINGLE LADIES

Maybe all this talk of forever has you reeling a little bit. Maybe you're fine on your own. Or maybe you're not—you know you have some work to do yet. Or maybe you have said yes to forever and you're feeling like that answer might have been premature. Or maybe "forever" was cut short for you. What then?

Listen, sis. Even if you feel invisible, God sees you. Even if you feel forgotten, God has not forgotten you and will never abandon you. Even if you feel unloved, God loves you and will never stop loving you. If you are experiencing loneliness or heartache or rejection or betrayal, rest assured that He won't waste a second of that pain.

Do you know what's new every single morning? God's mercies for you (see Lamentations 3:22-23). He has good plans for each of His children (see Jeremiah 29:11)—and that includes you. We don't have to know what the future holds to put God first in our lives. When we do that, the rest falls into place in His perfect timing.

Your Turn to Take a Breath

If you are married, think about your answer to the question "How did you two meet?" What role does your faith play in this important covenant? Are there any patterns you'd like to change in your relationship? If you aren't married, think about a couple whose marriage you respect. What aspects of their relationship are you drawn to? What do you think about the triangle analogy?

WHEN WE DO

THINGS IN THE

divine order,

THE REST TAKES

CARE OF ITSELF.

BLIND AMBITION

How Motherhood Turned My Life Upside Down

Pregnancy and motherhood are the most beautiful and
significantly life-altering events that I have ever experienced.

ELISABETH HASSELBECK

When Benjamin and I decided to start trying for kids, we were so excited. After a few slightly challenging years of marriage, we learned that we definitely loved each other. How much we *liked* each other fluctuated, and that was okay. It was thrilling to think that the shape of "us" was about to change, big time.

Together we'd dreamed and talked about what our family would look like. Suddenly it was all my brain would think about. I was happy. Hopeful. And I felt so grateful for what was to come.

If I could have seen then what our family would look like today, I would have fallen over in a dead faint. Me, driving a twelve-passenger van? Homeschooling with seven kids? That's not at all what I imagined.

No doubt your family looks a lot different from what you imagined too. Maybe you're single. Maybe you're raising kids on your own or you're in a blended family. Maybe your family is a group of close-knit friends. Maybe you're married, praying for children. Maybe you've adopted, or maybe you're fostering. Each family is unique, and that's a beautiful thing.

God loves surprising His children. And He has a great sense of humor!

PLANS FOR THE C-SUITE

I've always been ambitious, a dreamer. And I assumed that what the world told me was correct. To succeed, you do well in high school. You get accepted to college. You graduate with a degree and get a good job, and that job is the launch point into the rest of your life. You establish yourself in your career, get married, buy a house, maybe have a family, and send your kids to school so the whole thing can start over again.

My dad was my role model for business success. I had enough experience in sales to know that I excelled at it too. I sold Girl Scout cookies and, later, Cutco knives. I'm naturally persuasive, and I believe people prefer to buy from someone who believes in what they're selling.

If I believe in something, I want others to believe in it too. So I thought, *It's simple! I'll go into marketing. I'll work hard and get promoted, and soon I'll be running things. I'll get the corner office. I'll wear amazing tailored suits and gaze out my huge office window to see my sleek sports car in the parking space with my name on it.*

That was my vision. Sure, I'd have kids eventually. After I launched my successful business career, I'd go home to my little family. Together we'd take great vacations and make memories.

Sure enough, straight out of college I walked into a job at Home Depot's corporate headquarters in Atlanta. I'd been chosen as one of a handful of nationally recognized graduates for their elite two-year business leadership program.

On that first day, I felt proud. I was just twenty-three, but you couldn't tell me nothing. I had the security name badge. The suit. The swagger. The job with a great salary and all the perks. I was given access to some of the most important people in the corporation, and I was ready to learn everything I could from them. I figured I'd soon be in their ranks, living it up in the C-suite.

Soon it became clear to me that the others in the leadership program had figured out how to play the game. They wanted more access to the executives so they could promote their own careers. I wanted to learn too, but the politics didn't appeal to me at all. And while working hard had always been a big part of my life plan, the *appearance* of working hard was not. My peers stayed late at the office to get noticed. I was like, "Y'all are done with your work. Why are you staying? Go home."

Pretty soon I knew in my gut: *I'm not supposed to be here.* This was not the life I really wanted. This insight was confusing because, according to the world's rule-book, I had made it. This was what worldly success looked like—it checked all the boxes. I'd worked to accomplish all the things, so why didn't I feel like I was in the right place? Once the blinders fell off, I could clearly see that the measurements coming from the outside didn't matter to me. There had to be something else.

I didn't resign. I'm not a quitter. But once I admitted that worldly success wasn't going to satisfy me, I began to earnestly seek God's will. "Lord, if this isn't what You have planned for me," I said, "what is?"

I knew I would finish what I'd started at Home Depot, but I resolved that the corner office was no longer my goal. My goal was to discern the difference between the wisdom of the world and the wisdom that comes from God.

Two years after my leadership program ended, I married Benjamin and moved to Boston to live with him. This was just after his rookie year in the NFL. After a few years of figuring out how to live together and thrive together, we decided to try for kids. We'd already decided that one of us would be home with our children, and since Benjamin was playing football, I left my job at a nonprofit at Northeastern University to stay home with Baby #1, aka Grace.

It turns out that while it isn't the only thing I'm good at, being a mom is definitely my calling. Living out God's vision for me has been so much richer than my own. It's also infinitely more difficult. I'm not always the mom I'd like to be, but I keep trying. And I keep learning! Honestly, it's a good thing God didn't show me this life in advance because I wouldn't have felt capable of handling it all!

FROM POWER SUITS TO DIAPER GENIES

It turns out newborns are great theological teachers. Who knew?

I love hearing new moms talk about the books they're reading to get ready for the baby. I can't help but giggle to myself. You can read about it all you want—the reality is a whole new level!

Babies don't know *why* they cry. They just know something's not right. They will cry, scream, and kick until you figure out what needs doing. You can lovingly pick him up and coo and coax, but he's still gonna be upset until you supply what he needs—that thing he can't ask for yet.

I'm a lot like that, if I'm honest. I push, pull, and try so hard to make things happen. My need for control can be overwhelming. What I'm trying to do is learn from my children. What if I surrendered? What if I lifted up my open hands and said, "God, I don't know what I need, but You do. Help me."?

Before Grace came along, Benjamin and I had a good groove going. We had jobs outside the home we enjoyed. We were two adults living the dream. We were at work during the day, but we'd meet up for dinner, either at home or somewhere out to eat. Once a week Benjamin would cook. We'd share about our day—who we'd talked to, what we'd accomplished.

Then Grace was born, and it was like everything stopped for me. I was on a new planet where there were no other humans—at least nobody who could talk. Grace was born in the off-season, so Benjamin was around more than usual, but eventually he had to go back to work. I didn't. I fiercely loved this little person, but I was alone so much.

I'm a people person, and Baby Grace obviously couldn't talk. So I had all these conversations in my head. I started singing songs to her and talking to her almost constantly, just to hear the sound of someone's voice. Practically overnight, my life became unrecognizable to me.

It was a rude awakening. Everything was about the baby, as it should have been, but I wasn't prepared for my whole world and timeline to revolve around this little human. I couldn't do anything without taking into account when she was awake and when she was supposed to eat. Even a simple thing like when to take a shower or run to the grocery store had to be carefully timed. If she fell asleep in the car, it could throw us off course for hours. *Should I wake her or just stay with her in the car?*

I deeply loved her and felt so grateful to be her mom, and at the same time I had never felt so alone. I wondered if my education and my career and everything I'd worked for were meaningless. I felt like I was losing a part of myself because I wasn't sharing it with anyone. It was just me and this baby, cut off from the world. I couldn't help but wonder if this motherhood thing was going to be enough.

Even now, with this big family and the joy they bring me, a snide little voice in my head says, *This job is so beneath me.* When this attitude starts to get its claws into me, I recall how Jesus washed His disciples' stinky feet. Can you imagine how horrifying that must have been for those disciples—to have the God of the universe pick up their stinky feet and start washing them? It's not in the Bible, but I feel sure those guys hadn't just come from getting pedicures! At first Peter objected to having the Son of God stoop to such a menial task, but Jesus turned it around. He said, "[Now that I] have washed your feet, you also ought to wash one another's feet. For I have given you an example, that you also should do just as I have done to you" (John 13:14-15, ESV).

Whoa. Jesus always turns things upside down, doesn't He?

When I'm up late with one of the kids, my body tingling from exhaustion, I remember those words. When someone has a fever and I'm cleaning up vomit from the floor, frantically Lysoling everything to avoid an outbreak—I remember Jesus' model of servanthood. He has a way of making a proud girl humble.

ORIENTING LIFE AROUND
WHAT MATTERS MOST

The biggest thing our children need is to know that they belong to something bigger. They need to know that their Father rules the universe and that as children of the King, they are special and loved. At one point they'll make a decision for themselves about what they believe. Until then, it's on us as their parents to teach them the gospel.

> OUR CHILDREN NEED TO KNOW THAT THEY BELONG TO SOMETHING BIGGER.

I confess that part of me wants to lean on others to do this for me. I wonder if I can do it well enough or if a professional would do it better. Maybe a Sunday school teacher. Or a pastor. In my heart, though, I know this is just a cop-out. If I outsource something, I can blame someone else.

What if I get it wrong?

I've learned in teaching my children the gospel that I don't have to know it all. The point is that we learn together.

So how do we do that, practically?

God gives each of us certain gifts—we all bring our own strengths and weaknesses to the table. Regardless of our gifts, it's amazing what we learn ourselves while we're trying to teach. Through all of it, God is so kind, teaching us the entire time and helping us to go deeper with Him.

Can you imagine if, instead of starting out as babies, our children were given to us as fully grown teenagers? That would be such a challenge. Instead, we usually start with vulnerable babies who can't talk. We learn and grow together so that by the time the kids are older, we have the experience to navigate more sophisticated discussions and situations that arise.

When it comes to teaching our kids, it makes sense to start when they're little. When our oldest child was a toddler, I started by finding entertainment for her that was steeped in biblical principles. *Veggie Tales*, *Bibleman*—shows with a biblical worldview and a focus on teaching children God's Word. It wasn't just a matter of turning on a show to free me up for a few minutes of peace and quiet (which does happen, for sure). It's about creating an opportunity for conversation. I ask questions like, "Why does Larry act that way?" "Was that God's will?" "What did that mean?" Those stories provide doors into conversations about God. And the more we talk about God, the better.

Time in the car is also great for teaching kids about God. We listen to Bible stories like *Adventures in Odyssey* and Scripture-based kids' songs. Kids can memorize things so easily! To this day, they will sing Scripture songs they learned as little ones, long before they realized it was God's Word. While they were just singing and having fun, God's Word was being written on their hearts.

Ever notice how a kid can skin their knee and two days later it'll be healed? That same cut would take weeks to heal on you or me. Children are continually being renewed on a biological level in a way that we as adults aren't. Similarly, their minds absorb so many things.

That's God's design. It reminds me daily of my role as parent: to train them up.

You might think your kid can only learn in a Sunday school setting or with simplified versions of what Scripture says. Even our youngest will pick up something from family devotions. When we read a verse straight out of the Bible, our kindergartner will pick up some things, and our eleven-year-old will pick up others. It's amazing. What Hebrews 4:12 says is true: the Word is alive and active!

NO MORE CUTE PURSES

When I see a woman with a tiny purse, I feel a twinge of longing. I remember little purses!

These days I carry a bag. Anything you can need, I have in this bag. Hungry? Thirsty? Wet? Dirty? In need of a Band-Aid? An extra set of clothes? A wet wipe? I pretty much have it all in here.

As a mom of young kids, I spend a big part of every day planning for every contingency. Yet things still go wrong—things we couldn't have anticipated. There's the temper tantrum. The injury. The lost hat. The missing shoe.

NO MATTER WHAT I DO— OR DON'T GET DONE—I'M NOT REALLY IN CONTROL. GOD IS.

As a believer, I try to heed Jesus' advice as I get ready for what He has next for me: "Be dressed ready for service and keep your lamps burning, like servants waiting for their master to return from a wedding banquet, so that when he comes and knocks they can immediately open the door for him. It will be good for those servants whose master finds them watching when he comes" (Luke 12:35-37).

Being prepared is good. I just have to keep in mind that no matter what I do—or don't get done—I'm not really in control. God is. In the same chapter, Jesus says:

Do not worry about your life, what you will eat; or about your body, what you will wear. For life is more than food, and the body more than clothes. Consider the ravens: They do not sow or reap, they have no storeroom or barn; yet God feeds them. And how much more valuable you are than birds! Who of you by worrying can add a single hour to your life? Since you cannot do this very little thing, why do you worry about the rest?

LUKE 12:22-26

What a promise—God is ultimately the One who provides for us. And what a relief—it's not all up to me!

WE CAN DO HARD THINGS

In our family, we've had the pleasure—and the pain— of trying all the ways of educating our kids. We've done public schools, private schools, online learning, homeschooling—the works. It started when Grace was four, about to enter kindergarten. We visited this beautiful school—it had a garden and chickens and a beautiful building with friendly classrooms. I wanted to go there myself!

Afterward, when we got in the car, I said, "So, what do you think, Grace?"

She said, "Mommy, why can't you just teach me?"

I thought, *Hmm. Good question.*

That was the start of looking at what it might take to homeschool. I dove in! When the other kids were ready for school and we were still moving around for the NFL, it was pretty seamless to continue homeschooling.

When Grace was going into fourth grade, we moved back to New Orleans so Benjamin could play for the Saints. The kids went to the same school Grace and I had toured when she was four! It was a gift because that was the year I got pregnant with the twins. I don't know how it would have worked otherwise.

At this point I've seen the benefits and drawbacks of all the methods. We keep adjusting our approach to make sure it best fits our family's priorities and values, as well as the season of life we're in.

IN MY WEAKNESS, HE IS STRONG

If you haven't picked up on it yet, I'll just say it: I run a tight ship. In a house with seven kids, rules and timelines and protocols are nonnegotiable. Otherwise, our home would be in complete chaos.

Even when everything is going according to plan, a migraine headache can hit me out of the clear blue sky and send our day into a tailspin. Sometimes I can power through what I'm doing, whether I'm in the kitchen or helping the kids with a project, until I can take a break and lie down. But sometimes a headache comes on quickly and I can barely see straight, let alone walk.

If you've ever experienced a migraine, you know what I'm talking about. Such moments are demoralizing. These headaches make me feel so stinkin' weak—and I'm not a weak woman. I would give about anything to make them go away. Remember when Paul begged God to take the thorn in the flesh from him? I feel like that. But here's what Paul ultimately said: "For Christ's sake, I delight in weaknesses, in insults, in hardships, in persecutions, in difficulties. For when I am weak, then I am strong" (2 Corinthians 12:10).

I don't feel grateful for migraines. Still, I thank God for how He cares for me and mine when they hit. There is always some redemption—some way I can look back and see how He timed it so we had the help we needed at just the right time.

LIVING IN THE MOMENT

Some days feel like *Groundhog Day* at my house. It's basically the same day over and over—with nine people living under one roof. Last fall, five of our kids were working on schoolwork from their different stations around the house and the twins were basically just running around. Benjamin was working at home too, so it was all nine of us at home, 24-7. We realized Thanksgiving was about to roll around, and we hadn't left the house in weeks. We all needed a change of scenery. So we booked a little place to get away for a couple days and create a Thanksgiving adventure.

I'm thinking, *This is going to be awesome. We're going to make some good memories!* And you know me—I'm all about the food. So I dreamed up this Thanksgiving feast I wanted to prepare in advance—macaroni and cheese, greens, sweet potato casserole, pound cake. My plan was to cook all the food and bring it with us. That way we could just warm it up on Thanksgiving Day and voilà! Instant happiness!

So I got busy. I still had to pack for the eight of us (Benjamin packs his own clothes) and cook and run around after the twins to make sure nobody got hurt. Meanwhile, I got the kids set up with their online schoolwork while I tried to do a thousand things to get us ready for the perfect Thanksgiving getaway. All. The. Things.

All of a sudden one of the boys yelled at me from the other room. "Mommy, can you come here?"

Now during the day, I get a lot of questions, especially when it comes to school. I typically sit in the middle of the kids—they each have their own separate workstations. From there I can answer questions that arise during their school day. But this time I was moving all around the house. I had a lot going on.

I yelled from the kitchen, "Wait one second. I'm almost done here."

But my son was insistent. "Can you come now?"

"I'm busy!" I hollered. "What is the question?"

Still he called, "Can you please just come here?"

Y'all. I do not like being summoned. Who does, right? My patience was wearing thin. So I walked over to his desk and stood there, eyebrows raised. He nodded, like I was doing just what he wanted. I was thinking, *Do you know all I'm trying to get done? What is it that can't wait?*

Then I noticed all the faces on his laptop screen— the little, expectant faces of his classmates and the smiling face of his teacher. He was on a Zoom call. The teacher said, "Okay, class, has everyone had a chance to get something they're thankful for to share with the class?"

Oh. No.

There I was, annoyed and rushing to create something in the future—an imaginary happy family moment—and my son was simply trying to tell his class he was thankful for me. For *me*.

Just thinking of it gets me teary. What a reminder that sometimes we get an idea in our heads about what's important. We push things aside right now because we're anticipating what will be. That moment with my son taught me to not miss out on the present in my haste to create the future I want for us. What God has for me in this very moment is sufficient—even abundant! If I spend my life looking forward, I'll miss out on what He has for me now.

Now when I feel that urge to power into my own accomplishments and ambition, I take a deep breath. I slow down and try to be in the present moment—exactly where He's calling me to be.

Your Turn to Take a Breath

Prioritizing family looks different for every woman—
it's not a one-size-fits-all approach. Do you feel
supported in the balance between your family
and your responsibilities? When you need help,
where do you seek it? Recall a time when you were
best supported, and offer up gratitude. Consider
where else you might pursue additional backup,
whether that support is practical or emotional.

god loves

SURPRISING HIS CHILDREN.

AND HE HAS A

GREAT SENSE OF HUMOR!

CHAPTER 6

THE TALK

Straight Talk to My Peach Sisters

It is one thing to be awakened to injustice and quite another to be willing to be inconvenienced and interrupted to do something about it.

CHRISTINE CAINE

You may have noticed that *intentional* is a word I use a lot.

All relationships require intentionality. I'm intentional about my relationship with Benjamin, and together we are intentional about raising our family. Without intentionality—without purpose—chaos reigns.

When a baby is born, our every interaction with that child shows them what they can expect of us. We want them to know that we love them, that they can trust us.

As they grow, we educate them. We teach them to read, to do math. We teach them the Word of God and how to discern right from wrong.

You've heard about "teachable moments"? In our house, with seven kids, pretty much every waking moment is a teachable moment. There are ups and downs, of course, but most days I feel like we're making progress.

As Black parents—or "brown," as our kids say— trying to live intentionally, Benjamin and I don't get a pass when it comes to the difficult task of having "the Talk" with our kids. No, I don't mean the talk about sex, also known as "the birds and the bees." The Talk is about equipping our children for something far less pleasant. It's about honestly preparing them for the treatment they may receive simply because of the color of their skin.

The Talk goes something like this:

In this house, our expectations for you are clear.
You know what the rules are and what happens
when you don't obey them. But out there in
the world, things are different. You will have
to be especially careful when it comes to police
or authority figures. If you get pulled over by

a police officer, put your hands on the steering wheel, where they are clearly visible. Answer any questions with "Yes, sir" or "No, sir"—be extra respectful. Do exactly what you are told. Do not argue or talk back. Your life literally depends on how you handle this situation.

Is this conversation uncomfortable? Yes, extremely so. And if I'm honest, I resent having to say anything like this to my kids. It makes me angry. And it hurts. It's wrong that individuals in this country are automatically judged as more suspicious or dangerous than their lighter-skinned counterparts. And yet it happens all the time. Sometimes I wonder, *At what point will my precious twin sons go from being called "adorable" to being perceived as threats, simply because of the color of their skin?*

CLOSE TO HOME

When we were living in Baltimore, I turned on the news and heard that a Black man had been shot at close range by two armed police officers. That man's name was Alton Sterling. Soon this was all anyone could think about or talk about.

I remember feeling a strange mix of horror and relief. Horror, because Mr. Sterling had died at the hands of men who had sworn to protect the city's citizens, including him. And relief, because due to Benjamin's recent surgery on his Achilles, he wasn't able to drive for several weeks. Since all of Baltimore and really the entire US seemed gripped in unease and distrust, the last thing I wanted was for the man I loved most to get behind the wheel of a car. What if the police pulled him over? It was absurd to worry about him doing such a trivial activity like driving a car—and yet it was reality.

I don't share this to make my friends who are white—or "peach skinned," as our kids say—feel guilty or bad. I share it as a slice of reality. It's my reality. Our reality. And the reality of many of our friends and neighbors.

UNDER MY SKIN TOO

Racial injustice is not going away any time soon. Benjamin wrote beautifully about this tricky subject in his book, *Under Our Skin*. Since then, Benjamin and I have discussed this issue publicly and openly, as often as we can. We address racism on our podcast. And we speak about it often with our children.

Change starts in the heart, then takes hold in our homes, and we walk it out in our relationships.

I have to admit: every time we talk about race, I start feeling All. The. Feelings. It's not a simple topic to address. There aren't bullet points or instant fixes. There's a lot of tension around this issue, even with our close family members and friends.

So I return to my breathing.

Inhale.

Exhale.

And I remember Jesus' promise to send the Comforter, the Holy Spirit, who lives in me: "I will ask the Father, and he will give you another advocate to help you and be with you forever—the Spirit of truth" (John 14:16-17).

That same Holy Spirit lives in my brothers and sisters in Christ, regardless of skin pigmentation. Can't you feel the grace in that reminder? This truth emboldens me to speak with candor and love.

Racism is not an easy topic. But as sisters in Christ, we must talk about it—in a spirit of love and truth. Love is needed if we're going to stay engaged in relationship. And truth is the only way to push through to the other side. So let's take a big inhale. And exhale.

Here's my take.

DIGNITY ISN'T MINE TO GIVE OR TAKE

For me it starts with Genesis. God made people in His own image—*imago Dei*—to live in communion with

Him. We all have inestimable worth because we are all made in God's likeness.

The divisions that came after Creation are all due to sin. Jesus entered the human experience in a minority group—as a Middle Eastern, Jewish man—yet he wasn't about staying in any group, nor was he about keeping others out. Jesus ignored those kinds of power plays.

Over and over in the Gospels, Jesus refuses to dismiss anyone because of the world's standard for status. Jesus sees people—really sees them. As individuals. If we paint every person in a group with the same brush, we know for sure we are getting it wrong. No two people share the same story. Even "positive" prejudices (for instance, all Asians are smart or all Black people are fast) ignore the individual story. These "shortcuts" hurt more than they help.

Ultimately, it seems to me, the problem isn't color; the problem is when we value one color over another. Jesus laughed in the face of such divisions. If anything, Jesus got in trouble with the religious authorities for being too inclusive! Repeatedly in the Gospels religious folks accused Jesus of eating with sinners and tax collectors (see Mark 2:16-17; Matthew 9:11-13). He even struck up conversations with a Samaritan woman whose reputation was far from spotless. This was not the kind of behavior expected of a respected religious teacher ("rabbi"). Jesus saw the *imago Dei* in every person he encountered and treated them with dignity.

As a mom, I want my kids to be exposed to people and images of people who look like them and also those who look different from them. I want them to value the colorfulness of God's creation—of humanity. I want to encourage my children to keep their eyes open for opportunities to express gratitude to God for the colorfulness of humanity.

What kind of world would this be if we all looked just the same, if every flower were the same color, size, shape, and smell? What if the sky were always the same shade of blue, with no sunrises of gold or sunsets of pink, purple, and a hundred other hues?

> I WANT MY CHILDREN TO VALUE THE COLORFULNESS OF GOD'S CREATION.

I hope they will resist the urge to classify others into unhelpful categories of "us" and "them." We are all different—and that's something to rejoice about!

BETTER TOGETHER

Our sin gets between us and God, but Jesus bridged the gap for us at the Cross. So that separation has been healed, once and for all. The consequence of sin between us as humans, however, is more complicated.

It's God's desire that we will be united, as one body. That's not me trying to be a people pleaser and avoid conflict—it's straight from the Bible:

> Make every effort to keep the unity of the
> Spirit through the bond of peace. There is one
> body and one Spirit, just as you were called
> to one hope when you were called; one Lord,
> one faith, one baptism; one God and Father of
> all, who is over all and through all and in all
> (Ephesians 4:3-6).

Jesus prayed that we would be one as He and the Father are one (see John 17:11). The devil, on the other hand, is all about division. He wants to divide us and pick us off, one by one. He prowls around like a lion, looking for a way to cut us off from the body (see 1 Peter 5:8). He divides by using deception and false promises, by playing to our vanity and our desire for power. The devil seems to be working overtime right now. A quick scroll through the news or social media shows how much division there is in our world.

All of that is just noise—or, as Scripture puts it, "vanity of vanities" (Ecclesiastes, ESV). Only God can heal the divisions between us, but He invites us to participate in that healing. What we need now, sisters, is clarity. We need the wisdom of Scripture and the guidance of the Holy Spirit. Let's tap into those sources of wisdom and power as together we take a breath and have our own version of the Talk.

WHAT CAN I DO?

The passage in Galatians 5:22-23 that lists the fruits of the Spirit is one of my favorites. It talks about how we're transformed when we live through the Spirit: we become loving, kind, peaceful, patient. (My kids can sing a song about it, if you ask!)

But the verses right before this passage don't get nearly as much attention. In this passage, we find a list of acts of the flesh:

> The acts of the flesh are obvious: sexual
> immorality, impurity and debauchery; idolatry
> and witchcraft; hatred, discord, jealousy, fits of
> rage, selfish ambition, dissensions, factions and
> envy; drunkenness, orgies, and the like. I warn
> you, as I did before, that those who live like
> this will not inherit the kingdom of God.
>
> GALATIANS 5:19-21

Whoa. Think about that contrast for a minute. This list includes some really obvious sins to avoid, like witchcraft and idolatry. If you're like me, you probably read this passage and think, *Whew! I don't have to worry about that one!* But let's stop just a minute and notice that in this list of more than a dozen sins (some of which might make you blush), *four* involve divisions in the body of Christ:

- hatred
- discord
- dissensions
- factions

These are the things that divide us. What else is racism, if not hatred, discord, dissensions, and factions?

Fortunately, we have the Holy Spirit to combat these acts of the flesh and help us live lives rich in the fruit of the Spirit. The last one on the list, self-control, is especially relevant for this conversation. I'd challenge us as believers to use self-control to combat racism. To invite love and restoration into the body.

Here are three ways we can do just that.

Check Your Mouth

When it comes to the issue of racism, I find most people get defensive quick—as in zero to a hundred quick! We are often quick to point fingers at other people but slow to acknowledge and confess our own biases and the sin in our own hearts. True change happens only when we own our part of the brokenness in our world.

Proverbs 18:21 says, "The tongue has the power of life and death." That's pretty powerful stuff. Jesus Himself said, "I tell you that everyone will have to give account on the day of judgment for every empty word they have spoken" (Matthew 12:36). So when the issue of racism comes up, check your mouth. Inhale, exhale. Be careful not to point out the speck in your neighbor's eye when—who knows?—maybe you have a plank in yours. Jesus said, "First take the plank out of your own eye, and then you will see clearly to remove the speck from your [sister's] eye" (Matthew 7:5).

You may need to bite your tongue or the inside of your cheek. Then listen. I like how Stephen Covey sums it up in Habit 5 of *The 7 Habits of Highly Effective People*: "Seek first to understand, then to be understood." Makes sense, right? Don't just hear the words; listen so that you can view others as Jesus views them. So that you can love the way He loves.

Once you're ready to speak, here are a few things *not* to say to a Black woman.

- Please do not say racism doesn't exist. Just because a Black man held the highest office in America does not somehow eradicate racism in people's hearts.
- Do not say you are "colorblind." This may feel true to you—like you're making a statement of neutrality, claiming you don't have a bias. We all see color. As a Black woman, I need my people to see and acknowledge color, affording dignity to all. I need you to tell your kids about it so that when they see my kid getting treated differently because of their skin color, they will know it's not okay and they will speak up. Pretending there's no difference is just that—it's pretending. And that's not responsible or kind.
- Don't ask your colorful friends how they've been affected by racism. Sometimes people have asked me, with the best of intentions, to share my experiences of racism. They think hearing horror stories will create empathy, as if hearing firsthand accounts of racism will make it feel more real. I understand the heart behind this request, and

I respect it. What I want you to understand is that request is cruel. Asking someone to relive a trauma for your own benefit is unkind. It's painful for me to revisit moments of indignity, and frankly it's unnecessary. Instead, listen. Listen to each individual story, and let your friends choose to share it on their own terms. The act of listening affords respect and dignity. When we listen, we learn that no two people have the same story. Each of us is uniquely designed and loved by God. Every person deserves dignity and respect.

If you haven't experienced racial prejudice firsthand, praise God! I rejoice for you. In your abundance, you have the chance to speak up for those who do not have a voice. If you see injustice being done, speak up. As Martin Luther King Jr. put it, "To ignore evil is to become an accomplice to it."

Check Your Body

As you listen (without speaking), notice what you *feel* in your body when the issue of racial differences comes up. Pay attention to your body's reactions.

When you're alert to this, you may tune in to barely

perceptible thoughts or feelings, some of which you may have been oblivious to before. Maybe you'll notice your inclination to look away or cross to the other side of the street based on the way someone looks.

Acknowledge those feelings and thoughts. Own up to them. Shed a little internal light on them. Try pushing through your discomfort and admit that there's a way to do things a little differently. Then step into that new way.

My friend Ami was traveling to New York recently for work. When she sat down in her assigned seat on the plane, she noticed that the woman by the window wore a hijab. She felt her heart rate tick up a bit. She didn't say hello at first.

Ami took a beat and asked herself why she was feeling uncomfortable and realized that she'd only seen a woman dressed that way in movies and on TV. In those roles, such women were portrayed as the enemy. Pushing through her discomfort, Ami greeted her seatmate with a quiet smile.

Later, when the flight attendant offered drinks on the flight, she and her seatmate exchanged a few words. As they began to talk, Ami found they had some things in common. Both were traveling for work. Both had young families at home. They were even reading the same bestselling book. At their destination, they parted cordially. What might have been an uneventful flight turned into a breakthrough for my peach-colored friend.

I've had similar experiences myself. I can't tell you the number of times a simple conversation has changed an initial belief I've had about someone else—or someone has had about *me*. I've felt it: someone who was on guard with me started relaxing, smiling, and becoming engaged in real conversation. And it can start with something as simple as initiating a conversation.

Check Your History

Think back to when you were a kid and you first heard something negative about someone whose skin color was different from your own. How old were you? Was it a joke? Was it a story? Who did you hear it from? Maybe it was a family member or a teacher or a classmate. Recall what that person meant to you. What did their words and their actions teach you?

As a child, you were learning how to see people, how to value people. You came into this world innocent. You learned what's acceptable or expected by the people who taught and influenced you—for better or for worse. Racial prejudice isn't something we're born with; we learn it. It's a sin that took root somewhere, and that root needs to be discovered if we aim to get rid of it.

As with any type of sin, we have to uncover where it started if we want to be set free. We need to peel the onion back to reveal layer upon layer of learned behavior. When we confess sins such as pride, jealousy, and control, it's not like, poof, they're gone the moment we confess. Racism is no different. It's a sin that hurts other people and keeps us from being the people God has called us to be.

This task of uprooting racism is hard work. But it's important. It's impactful. And it's for the glory of the Lord and His Kingdom.

Check Your Heart

King David was human, and he messed up like we do. Scripture tells us that David was a man after God's own heart (see 1 Samuel 13:14). What I admire most about David isn't his leadership or the seemingly impossible battles he won or the giant he took down. I admire him most for this prayer: "Search me, God, and know my heart; test me and know my anxious thoughts. See if there is any offensive way in me, and lead me in the way everlasting" (Psalm 139:23-24).

Let's be bold like David and ask God to show us "any offensive way" in us, especially when it comes to the way we treat one another. On this side of heaven, there will always be gunk that needs to be removed so God's glory can shine through. It may be uncomfortable, but it gives me peace to know that the Comforter will be there when God reveals things about us that need to be changed.

Loving our neighbor isn't easy. But this command is at the very core of the faith—the second greatest commandment. It's second only to loving the Lord our God with all we are (see Matthew 22:37-40). I truly believe there's only one way to love our neighbor, and that's one person at a time.

GOD OF JUSTICE

Make no mistake: God cares about justice. Take a look at what the Word says about God's character: "He is the Rock, his works are perfect, and all his ways are just. A faithful God who does no wrong, upright and just is he" (Deuteronomy 32:4). Jesus, who lived in full communion with God and is Himself God, didn't grasp at power. Instead, He lifted up those without power.

> WE HAVE AN OBLIGATION TO RIGHT WRONGS WHEN WE SEE THEM.

As believers, we have an obligation to right wrongs when we see them. It's the foundation of who we are as the body of believers. The book of James demonstrates the essentials of our faith, especially how the faithful need to take action.

> Suppose a . . . sister is without clothes and daily food. If one of you says [to her], "Go, I wish you well; keep warm and well fed," but does nothing about [her] physical needs, what good is it? In the same way, faith by itself, if it is not accompanied by action, is dead.
>
> JAMES 2:15-17

This is a call to action, sister. It's my prayer that we'll hear and act on it. One day justice will reign. Until then, we do what we can to bring God's justice to our world. One heart at a time. One interaction at a time.

Your Turn to Take a Breath

What happens to your body when talk turns to racism? Think of a time you encountered a difficult racial situation you wished you'd handled differently. What would you do or say differently next time? Make a list of things you could say and do (or teach your children to say and do) when you see injustice and racism.

THERE'S ONLY ONE WAY TO

love our neighbor,

AND THAT'S ONE PERSON

AT A TIME.

CHAPTER 7

PRAYER

As Long as I Have Breath

Because he bends down to listen,
I will pray as long as I have breath!

PSALM 116:2, NLT

Did you like to play hide-and-seek as a child? I did—it's a classic! I can still remember the thrill of shouting, "Not it!" and the hustle to find a place to hide, trying to quiet my breath so I'd be as still and silent as I possibly could. I remember trying not to giggle when I heard the seeker's steps and the adrenaline of racing to home base. So fun, right?

There's a hide-and-seek memory that's not as fun—one we tend to forget as adults. It's that sinking feeling when you've found a great hiding spot and some time has passed and . . . you're still hiding. You start to think, *Wait. Am I the last one hiding? What if nobody finds me? What if I'm alone here forever?*

It's such a lonely feeling! With hide-and-seek, that feeling doesn't last long, because for the game to end, everybody has to be found! But as adults, we still get that sinking feeling sometimes. We wonder, *Am I all alone here? Has everyone made it home but me?* In dark moments, we wonder, *Am I even worth discovering? Am I worth finding and being seen?*

CHILD, GOD SEES

The good news of the gospel is that the God of the universe pursues each of us individually. The omniscient, all-powerful Creator longs for a relationship with us. He wants it so much that He sent his Son to draw us back to Himself.

Jesus is the ultimate Seeker. To illustrate the depths of His commitment, He told a story about a shepherd whose sheep roamed off from the safety of his care. All alone, a sheep would face certain death, whether from predators or from dangerous terrain. In the story, the shepherd leaves the rest of the flock—the other ninety-nine—to rescue the lost sheep (see Matthew 18:12).

Finding that lone sheep is not a game for Jesus. Oh no. He has already overcome the world, y'all. He seeks out of love. He longs for relationship with us. His desire is that we would know the Father as intimately as He does.

This side of heaven, the best way to know and be in relationship with God is to come out of hiding and pray "without ceasing" (1 Thessalonians 5:17, ESV). This may sound like an impossible aspiration. With all our responsibilities and everything on our to-do lists, how could we find ten minutes of uninterrupted time, let alone every minute of every day?

I don't think this means we're literally on our knees all the time. So what is this verse actually talking about? The details may look different for each of us, depending on our personalities and our stage of life. But here's a glimpse into what it looks like for me.

A RELATIONSHIP WITH THE FATHER

God is the Creator and King of the universe, worthy of all respect and honor. So the idea of praying to Someone like that can be intimidating. Maybe that's why some people feel the need to use fancy words when they pray, peppering their prayers with "Thou" and "Thy" even though they would never in a million years talk that way in real life! That intimidation factor may keep us from prayer altogether. We picture God sitting on a throne, judging us. The shame or fear we feel keeps us from real intimacy with God.

Jesus, the Son of God, presented a very different image of God's disposition toward us. He paints a picture of a father who rushes out to greet his wandering, philandering child. Jesus told a story about a son who finally returns home after turning his back on his father and squandering his inheritance. Instead of lecturing him or demanding restitution, the father shows unconditional love for his son: "While he was still a long way off, his father saw him and was filled with compassion for him; he ran to his son, threw his arms around him and kissed him" (Luke 15:20).

How undignified is that—running to embrace your stinky kid? That's the picture Jesus painted of God embracing us, even when we turn our backs on Him!

Because of Jesus, we bear our Father God's name. We are His kids. Jesus called God Abba, which is another word for Daddy. And He didn't just do this once—Jesus regularly used this term of endearment. At the time, it would have been

> BECAUSE OF JESUS, WE BEAR OUR FATHER GOD'S NAME. WE ARE HIS KIDS.

considered the height of presumption to address God on such familiar terms. The religious rulers of the day didn't like it much, yet it was totally accurate. What's more, we're invited to address God through Jesus that way too: "The Spirit you received does not make you slaves, so that you live in fear again; rather, the Spirit you received brought about your adoption to sonship. And by him we cry, "*Abba*, Father" (Romans 8:15).

Take a minute to let that sink in, sis. We get to call the God of the universe Daddy! As Jesus' disciples, we are God's own children.

AT HOME WITH HIM

Imagine waking up in the morning and going into the kitchen for your morning coffee, smoothie, or tea. Your kid is there and doesn't say "Good morning" or even look up to acknowledge you. You try to get in their face, but they simply act like you're not there. That would be so hurtful, wouldn't it?

God wants us to come out of our hiding place to be with Him—all day, every day. His invitation to be with Him is always open. He welcomes us to talk with Him, walk with Him, and crawl into His outstretched arms and rest.

That's the Daddy we get to know and serve.

BEING "WITH"

We are God's found kids—it's as simple and glorious as that. That means we get to be with Him. When I think about being with our heavenly Father, it's not about what we say or do; it's about a way of being. It's a way to *be* with the One who loves us most in the world.

Communication isn't just words. It's more complex than that—in a good way! Research reveals that we communicate primarily in three ways: with words, with body language, and with utterances.[1] This is a relief, because if we had to get the words just right when talking to God, I would feel so much pressure! The reality is that God wants us to show up, with our whole, authentic selves. He's not looking for a performance; He wants our hearts. Prayer isn't a "one and done" deal. It's about an ongoing relationship.

PRAYER ISN'T A "ONE AND DONE" DEAL. IT'S ABOUT AN ONGOING RELATIONSHIP.

Imagine if someone showed up at your door and said, "Remember me—your classmate from kindergarten? I'm whisking you off for a quick trip to Vegas. I'm driving—we'll take your car."

You'd be like, "What? That's nonsense! We don't have a relationship! We haven't spoken in years, let alone spent time together!"

You'd be wise not to trust this person. Shared life is key to bonding and building trust.

The same is true of our relationship with God. The more time we spend with Him, the more we get to know His character and His heart, and the more we learn to trust Him—with the big things and the small things. My encouragement to you is that we don't have to filter with God. He can take it all: our doubts, fears, anxieties, joy, dreams, concerns. Whatever is on our hearts.

For me, praying without ceasing looks like starting the day with a greeting to acknowledge God's presence. It's the first thing I do when I open my eyes each morning, and it's a great way to set my heart right for the day.

As the day goes on, I like to have checkpoints with the Lord. This doesn't have to be formal or complicated— it could just be a quick prayer for patience when I'm about to lose my cool with one of my kids or a prayer for wisdom when I'm talking to a friend. It's a relief to know that God is interested in hearing from me at any time. There's no problem too big for Him to handle and no worry too small for Him to care about.

GOD WILL MEET YOUR NEEDS

As the COO of my big family, I'm a big planner. I wake up thinking about our family's needs. *What does*

Benjamin have going on? Which kids need new socks or underwear replaced, and in what size? What school assignments need attention? Which sports events or rehearsals do we need to get to? Do I have what it takes to make our meals on time and healthy?

God promises to provide for all our needs. Scripture promises, "My God will supply every need . . . according to his riches" (Philippians 4:19, ESV). Jesus taught this lesson over and over, pointing out how God cares for the birds and the lilies—and how much more He cares for His kids (see Luke 12:27-31)!

Jesus describes the father-love of God this way:

Which one of you, if his son asks for bread,
will give him a stone? Or if he asks for a fish,
will give him a snake? If you, then, though you
are evil, know how to give good gifts to your
children, how much more will your Father in
heaven give good gifts to those who ask him!

MATTHEW 7:9-11

Knowing this is God's heart, I can have the boldness to ask Him for what I need. I ask for intervention in my relationships. I ask that my kids will be honest with me. I pray that Benjamin and I can have open dialogue with them about what they're hearing and seeing. I pray for discernment, and I ask the Holy Spirit to give me the words to say when I speak with family and friends. Since God has promised to meet my needs, I can bring my concerns to Him rather than fretting about them and trying to meet these needs myself.

This morning, my first thought when I woke up was, *God, please give me the energy to throw my feet over the side of this bed so I can get up and work out with my husband.* My next thought was, *Now will you help me keep my temper even though I'm still mad about last night?* This is what it looks like to rely on God for my every need!

Because God loves me, He answers my prayers. Sometimes not immediately—but often right then! He also doesn't answer every prayer the way I want Him to, but He answers in the way that is ultimately best for me.

Talking with God makes us aware of how He is constantly at work, providing for us in the moment. And working His plans for good.

THANKS AND PRAISE

God knows how our minds work. As our Creator, He knows well how our brains get fixated on our own wants and needs. I think that's why again and again in Scripture, we're commanded to praise—to look up from our puddle of tears and self-focus so we can see the good He's doing and has already done. When we do, we can put things in perspective. We can realize that this moment will pass. And we can do so from the vantage point of eternity.

Gratitude doesn't minimize our pain, needs, or desires; it right-sizes them.

Scripture is clear about the command, the invitation, to be grateful and praise God: "Rejoice always, pray continually, give thanks in all circumstances; for this is God's will for you in Christ Jesus" (1 Thessalonians 5:16-18). Psalm 150:6 says, "Let everything that has breath praise the LORD. Praise the LORD." Even though my mind agrees with this, I'm not always in the mood. It's a lot like drinking enough water or waking up early to work out—I have to will myself to do it. But in the long run, I'm always glad I did.

One practical strategy that helps me cultivate gratitude is to start with a top-ten list. It's a low bar to clear, truly. I start with the basics, like hot water for my shower. Once I start rolling, I begin to realize just how much I have to be thankful for—both big things and the little things I tend to take for granted.

"WHAT ARE YOU UP TO?"

My mom came from Atlanta recently to look after our kids for a couple of days while Benjamin and I went out of town. Knowing that she'd have a lot of questions, I wrote out a schedule of what all our kids needed to do, where they needed to be, and what to feed them over the course of the forty-eight hours Benjamin and I would be gone. Y'all, the list was five pages long. That's a *lot*, right?

I know I'm not alone in having a full plate. I'm sure you feel the same: as women, we are responsible for a lot!

For me, a day can get out of hand so easily. A saving grace for me is to remember what the Bible tells me to do: "Commit to the LORD whatever you do, and he will establish your plans" (Proverbs 16:3).

Whoa. When I invite God into my plans, I hold them loosely, believing that He has a better handle on my life than I do. Committing my plans to Him means subverting my own ego to God's glory. And God does not fail! This is such a relief to me—and a grace.

LISTENING

I love to go to a nice dinner. However, my idea of the worst night ever is going to a meal where the other person talks without ever inviting me into the conversation. Have you ever been there? The other person launches into their pet topic, and you never manage to get a word in edgewise. If it weren't so disappointing, it might be almost humorous, right?

I confess that I can be guilty of this—especially in my prayer life. What would it look like to make sure we listen as much as we talk in our relationship with God? Check out what Mother Teresa says: "I always begin my prayer in silence, for it is in the silence of the heart that God speaks. God is a friend of silence—we need to listen to God because it's not what we say but what He says to us and through us that matters."[2] I'm trying to make this a practice, too. It's especially good for me to read from Scripture and then sit and breathe a while to see what God is saying specifically to me.

God is sovereign—He knows everything already. Revelation 1:8 reminds us that God is the Alpha and Omega, who is, who was, and who is to come. God doesn't need us to tell Him anything. He already knows. It's not for His benefit that He asks us to bring him our concerns, requests, and praise. It's for ours.

WHEN WORDS FAIL

Sometimes I just don't have the words to express my thoughts or feelings. But hiding from God in those times is the last thing I want to do!

When words fail me, I have two hacks. One is to go to the words of a psalm or a worship song to help me express what I'm experiencing—even if those feelings are uncomfortable or painful. We've recently taught our kids the prayer that Jesus taught His disciples in the Our Father. Praying that when I don't have words of my own is a gift.

The other hack sounds almost too easy to be effective. It's simply saying the name of Jesus as a prayer. Sometimes things with all our kids get crazy. Especially if I'm tired, all those words and thoughts fill my mind to overflowing. At those times, whispering Jesus' name brings such a sense of communion and calm.

When I'm truly at a loss to connect with the Lord in prayer, I remember Romans 8:26: "We do not know what we ought to pray for, but the Spirit himself intercedes for us through wordless groans." *Groans*—I love that word. Sometimes that's literally what I'm doing, y'all. Groaning. God reminds me that I'm not alone and He's still in charge, working for good.

PRAYING SCRIPTURE

Over the years, I've learned to pray Scripture over my family—my husband and each of our kids. For instance, if my child is feeling anxious, I'll pray Psalm

46:1-3. "God, you are Grace's refuge and strength, an ever-present help in trouble. Remind her of your presence and cast out her fear."

I also pray for the people my children encounter on the daily. I pray for their teachers. I pray for their friends. And I pray for their enemies or those who might hurt them.

One evening my daughter came home from soccer tryouts in tears. A girl at practice had told her she couldn't see my daughter's sweat because she's Black. After the tears and a long conversation with my daughter and the rest of our kiddos, Benjamin and I prayed for that little girl, using Scripture to speak truth and grace over the situation. Lo and behold, they were placed on the same team, and by the end of the season, they became friends.

Going to Scripture to help me pray for my loved ones reminds me of a profound truth: God is my source. Not my husband, my girlfriends, or my parents. God knows me better than I know myself. He comforts me and guides my steps. And He can watch over my family better than I can.

TAKE A DEEP BREATH

Sister, I urge you to relax into a life of prayer. It isn't another thing to add to an already overwhelming to-do list. It's that sense of relief you've been looking for—that peace we all need.

Just imagine it: the all-powerful, all-compassionate Father patiently waits for you to enter His peaceful presence. From His mighty throne, He extends His strong arms and invites you to rest there. I can't say it better than Paul, who put it this way: "Let us then with confidence draw near to the throne of grace, that we may receive mercy and find grace to help in time of need" (Hebrews 4:16, ESV).

Your Turn to Take a Breath

Even now you are being seen by "the God who
sees" (Genesis 16:13). Take a moment to close
your eyes and meet with God. For a few moments,
don't worry about having an agenda; simply *be* in
His presence.

gratitude

DOESN'T MINIMIZE OUR

PAIN, NEEDS, OR DESIRES;

IT RIGHT-SIZES THEM.

CHAPTER 8

SISTERS

Who Are Your Dark-Alley Friends?

You know you are with true friends when they lift,
encourage, correct, and then spur you on.

LISA BEVERE

As a result of our moves, I've been blessed to have developed friendships with women all over the country. With every move, I felt a divine assurance that there would be someone in that place I needed and someone who needed me. And that's been the case.

I often refer to my "dark-alley friends." These are the women I can rely on to stick with me through the tough times. These are the women who stand with me, no matter what.

God knew exactly what I was going to need when He sent me my New Orleans sister. I wasn't sure what He was up to at the time, but He orchestrated my meeting her in response to a desperate cry of my heart. In His perfect timing, God provided what I needed, even when I didn't know quite what to ask for.

Let me back up to give you the full story.

When Benjamin and I got married, he was playing for the New England Patriots. I thought he'd be in the NFL for maybe five years. Sixteen seasons later, it's safe to say that I underestimated! Benjamin knew his job was to play football, but his purpose was to fulfill God's assignment for his life—both in the NFL and for our family. I trust him to lead our family because I know he's constantly seeking God's direction.

Early in our marriage, we decided we wouldn't split up our family for football. Regardless of where the NFL took him, we pledged that we would move wherever he played. Even when his schedule was heavy during the season, our desire was to all be together.

We began our marriage in Boston when he was playing with the Patriots. After we had Grace, we left dear friends there and moved to Cleveland so Benjamin could play for the Browns. There we added Naomi and Isaiah to the family—and I was pregnant again. Three kids in three years. In all honesty, I was ready for my husband to retire. There was nothing I wanted more than to settle into what I'd imagined as our forever home.

I longed for a house that would fit our family perfectly—a place where we could build swing sets and hang pictures and tear down walls if we wanted to. I wanted to be able to put down roots that would run deep. It may sound silly, but I wanted a new house with a new toilet where my butt was the first one on it. I dreamed of a place where we weren't temporary residents but were there for good. In my heart, I wanted a community where we could be seen and loved just as we were.

I could hardly wait for my husband to be with us instead of working and traveling so much. I didn't want to have to worry about his health and potential injuries anymore. I wanted to focus on raising our growing family together. And frankly, I felt lonely a lot of the time. Even with all those littles, I felt isolated.

Benjamin sought the Lord's will and came to the conclusion that he hadn't finished his assignment from God in the NFL yet. So when I was nine months pregnant with Judah (our fourth child), my husband, who had already been in the NFL for nine years, got a call from the New Orleans Saints.

I didn't know what was going to happen, but I knew free agency was about to start, so anything was possible. Our lease was about to expire. At thirty-seven weeks pregnant, I didn't know where we'd be moving, but I knew we were moving out. Benjamin took the two oldest girls on a special trip, which gave me some time and space to pack. He called me that night, excited. He said, "Guess what? We're moving to New Orleans." The Saints had offered him a three-year contract. My longing to put down roots would have to wait.

Benjamin and the girls flew back after he told me the news. I met them at the airport, picked up the girls, and kissed my husband goodbye. He got on the next flight to New Orleans, signed the contract, then flew home to Cleveland that night. I went into labor three days later and had Judah. That weekend Benjamin returned to NOLA to find a house to rent, then flew back to Cleveland on Sunday. Time to go!

Judah was only two weeks old when the movers came. The big purple truck pulled up our street, and Naomi said, "They're here! They're here!"

The same movers who had moved us before were joking with me. "Wasn't there just the one when we moved y'all here?"

Now we had four kids under four. After the movers

left in the truck, we boarded a plane to New Orleans with our four littles. We had to leave our Yorkie, Nala, behind with the trainer. I might have cried if I weren't so exhausted.

I was feeling the urge to nest big-time. And yet how could I? All I could do was unpack between feedings and playing with the other kids. Given that Benjamin had signed up for three more years, we were at least that many years away from our "forever home." I'd made a few treasured sisters in Cleveland, and now we were leaving them, too. Our little crew was breaking up as a result of NFL trades, free agency, and retirement. It felt like we were nomads.

I was committed to supporting Benjamin and felt we were doing the right thing for our family. Even so, I privately cried out to God. We'd been blessed with this healthy, big family, so why did I feel so lonely? And I was so tired! True rest eluded me. It didn't help that Benjamin started training with the team just a few days after we arrived.

With everything else in our life so scattered, I felt God leading us to worship. As soon as we got to New Orleans, I knew we needed to plug into a church community so I could recharge and refuel before Benjamin started training camp. I needed a place that preached the Word and also had great parking, since I would be going alone with the kids during the season.

Benjamin and I took all four kids to a number of churches before we landed at what would be our home church. The first Sunday there, Benjamin was pushing little Judah, just three months old, in his Orbit stroller. If you've never seen an Orbit, I can tell you, they're unique looking. Well, there was a couple that had the same kind.

When Benjamin rolled up with Judah, this guy said, "Hey, looks like we have the same stroller."

The two of them were talking when I walked up with the other three kids. At some point during the conversation, our family had been invited to dinner after church. Benjamin agreed right away, which is very unlike him.

I said, "Let me get your wife's number, and I'll call her." To be honest, I felt protective—what if we got there and this dude pulled out some jerseys for Benjamin to sign and we were stuck with some crazy football fans? Plus, I wasn't sure I had the energy. Bringing four kids into a stranger's home can be a lot of work! What if their house wasn't kid friendly—what if they had all white couches and my kids ruined them?

But then his wife walked over and said, "Please come! Bring your munchkins and we'll order pizza."

Something in me said to go for it, and I immediately felt so welcomed into their home. The couches *were* white, which made me nervous, but our new friends made us feel so at ease. She was a great hostess—probably the best I know. Benjamin clicked with her husband, and our kids had a great time together. I don't think they even talked about football, much less pulled out any jerseys. So I took a breath and enjoyed our time together.

Not long after that, they invited us to their Bible study and prayer group. That small group became a lifeline for me during our time in New Orleans.

HEART'S CRY

My longing for a forever home wasn't wrong—it was put there by God. And He will fulfill that longing someday. For sure it will be satisfied in heaven. But looking back, I can see that what I longed for was about more than four walls. It was about being seen and known—a basic human longing. And for moms in the thick of raising little ones, this need can be intense. Children are a blessing from God, no doubt, but they can be bottomless pits of needs and wants! As mommas, we give, give, give all day, and sometimes this can leave us feeling empty.

In most places we'd lived before, I had one or maybe two close friends. I was reluctant to really put down roots, waiting for the perfect time. The problem in football life is that people get traded or released, or they retire, and every year looks different. I learned to self-protect.

Looking back, I can see that I hadn't learned to trust God with my heart. I was worried about what I'd lose when we had to move again. But now God was working in me, pushing me out of my comfort zone. I didn't need to be in the "right place" to put myself out there. God would provide for my needs regardless of where we were—or even how long we'd be there. God was teaching me that every soul around me has been placed there by Him.

I've decided that even if we move every year, I'm going to put myself out there and meet people. Benjamin's not the only one on assignment from God! Each place has a woman or group of women I need and women who need me. The risk of friendship, of vulnerability, is worth it. Even if that friendship is for the day, it's worth it.

SURPRISE FRIENDSHIPS

It's natural to walk into a room and look around for the folks who look like us. Maybe that's because we think they're most likely to embrace us. But when we develop relationships with ladies from different backgrounds, perspectives, and life experiences, our lives are enriched.

Not long ago, as a surprise birthday present, Benjamin gathered my friends from across the country for a girls' weekend. I was blown away. Looking around that room, it would be difficult to guess what these women had in common. We're all different ages and ethnicities. Some are NFL girls, some are church girls. Some are young moms, some are single ladies—all the stories were represented! What's amazing is that even though I was the only common human thread, once we were together, we all got along like we'd been friends for years.

None of this was a surprise to God. He had been setting up this scenario all along. It was special to me to notice how each of these friends had brought unique, God-given contributions to my life.

MEET IN REAL LIFE

It can be tempting to think of scrolling through our social media feeds as a sort of friendship. We wish people a happy birthday on Facebook or like their most recent post, and it feels like a connection. Let's do a gut-check on that, though. Is that really putting yourself out there as a friend?

Social media can be a good diversion, and it has some upsides. But is it fair to call the people who observe your life from a distance "friends"? People who see your social media know about one percent of what's going on in your life. Even if I spend hours scrolling through my friends' updates on social media, I see only a sliver of what's going on in their lives—and all of it is curated so I just see the pretty parts, the notable moments. That's not the whole story.

In our culture, we've swallowed the lie that the more widely recognized someone is, the more valuable they are. Apps on our phones calculate value based on the number of followers and likes. But it's all smoke and mirrors, y'all.

Real friends do real life together—no filter, no makeup. They take walks together, call and text each other, celebrate kids' birthdays and milestones together, show care for each other. Do we all need to get off social media? Not necessarily. I'm just saying let's be real. And let's take off the rose-colored glasses and see each other for who we really are.

PUTTING PEOPLE ON A PEDESTAL

I'm quick to spot and admire women of excellence, yet I'm careful not to put anyone on a pedestal. God's Word says that all of us are in need of salvation and fall short of God's glory (see Romans 3:23). It's not like anyone has it all figured out. When someone impresses me, I try to ask myself, *What is it I admire here? What can I learn from her?* Figuring out the answers matters for a couple of reasons.

1. It's intentional. This way we're not just elevating someone to superhuman levels; we're thinking through their actions so we can learn from them. So, for instance, if I say, "Wow, Nadia is so present when we're together. She didn't look at her phone one time during our lunch. That makes me feel honored and cared for," I can take that thoughtfulness and bring it into my own life.

2. Isolating the traits we appreciate in others helps us avoid the tendency to idealize the rest of their life. People are human. We're all works in progress. In all of our lives—even in someone who seems to have it all together—there are aspects we struggle with and others we have down pat.

We can't have a true friendship with someone when they're on a pedestal. But when we're real with them—and when we invite them to be real with us—it can create the foundation for a mutually fulfilling friendship.

WHAT WE BRING

All our moves have taught me the importance of putting down roots in the right place. My roots have to be deep in my faith and in the knowledge of God, not in my house or the city I live in. Those things can change at any time.

Even so, it's no good to do life alone. We were created for community, sister. Go back to the beginning, in the Garden. God breathed life into Adam, which meant Adam was walking around with God's own breath in his lungs. That's when God declared that it's not good for humans to be alone. Even in a perfect world, we need each other.

Rarely in real life are the packs of friends like those fictional "friend groups" we see on TV and in movies. You know, there's always a funny one, a smart one, one who's always talking about sex . . . well, maybe there's some truth to that one. It's impossible for any one friend or friend group to meet every need. Only God can do that. When I find myself wishing a friend were everything I want her to be, I try to check myself and bring that desire to God.

Think about the women you've chosen to do life with. Each one is God's "workmanship, created in Christ Jesus for good works" (Ephesians 2:10, ESV). Each of us has something unique to give—and we may not even know what we're bringing. One gift of friendship is learning the unique blessings and talents you have to offer.

Maybe you'll see yourself or your friends in the following descriptions.

Memory Keepers

Some women have been there in key moments of my life that turned out to be milestones. Not long ago, a couple of friends and I were sharing a meal, and Courtney told a story about me from twenty years ago, when I was an intern. I had forgotten that part of who I used to be. Friends often lovingly reflect to us who we are—and who we've been.

Cheerleaders

When I'm in need of a confidence boost, I know what to do. When I talk to Arin and Gia, it's like getting a B_{12} shot. How this works is a mystery to me. All I know is that when I hang up the phone, I feel like Superwoman! They have the gift of encouragement, and they know how to make me laugh—like, tears-streaming-down-my-face laughter.

Truth Speakers

God has uniquely equipped some of my friends to get into my stuff and call me out! I don't want everyone in my life to do this all the time. That would be too much conflict! But there are some women I trust who will do this for me occasionally. I have learned that I need these friends. They know my heart, and they know how to call me out in a way that won't put me on the defensive. As the Bible says, "Iron sharpens iron" (Proverbs 27:17). Truth spoken in love is such a gift.

Prayer Warriors

There have been times when I was so hurt or sad that words wouldn't come. Or when I was pounding on heaven's door so loud and so long that I ran out of energy. In those times, I've been blessed to have faithful friends who come alongside me and pray. Shahrzad has an incredible gift of prayer. Her words, whether by text or in person, calm my soul and help put things into perspective. As Scripture says, "the prayer of a righteous person is powerful and effective" (James 5:16).

Up-the-Road Friends

I celebrate when I meet a woman who has already navigated the road I'm currently traveling. At first this can feel like, "Oh! What a coincidence!" But I've learned that this isn't something to be taken lightly. Experience is the best teacher, so if someone else has already walked through what I'm walking through, I should lean in and take notes! As Proverbs 13:20 says, "Walk with the wise and become wise." When a friend has valuable wisdom to share, I listen. That way I may be able to avoid gaining the same wisdom the hard way!

Adventure Lovers

Some women are good at cooking up adventures. You know the type—the ones who invite you to their book club, plan a girls' weekend, or share tickets to a concert. It's no secret that I'm the planner for my friend groups. I love having girls who want to go, will do what's necessary to save the date, and enjoy being together. It also helps when the guys encourage us to go—and agree to watch the kiddos. My adventure lover friends bring much-needed joy to my life!

Walking Pinterest Boards

God gifts some women with a deep knowledge of DIY and a capacity for making things beautiful. One day I hope to work this muscle more than I do now. Holidays are a favorite time of year for me. That said, we haven't lived in one place long enough for us to have traditions around decorating our house. We had a tree with all the kids' decorations on it, but I had something different in mind—I wanted a "mommy tree." That's how I ended up in Hobby Lobby one fall, literally walking in circles with an empty cart, confused by all the choices. I called up my girlfriend Whitney, and she walked me through what I needed. Those decorations turned out pretty good, if I do say so myself—thanks to my crafty friend.

Casserole Sisters

There are certain women who can be counted on to bring a casserole or a full four-course meal (including homemade dessert!) when someone is sick or has a baby. Sometimes these women even prepare you a meal just because they love you! I've been on the receiving end of these gifts when things were tough. Some women are better equipped than others to grieve with you over a miscarriage, to hold your hand in the ER, or to listen while you pour out your heart about a hurting loved one. I'm so grateful for my friend Tamela. She has even sent her famous fried catfish and homemade Rice Krispies treats overnight to our family "just because." These women shine in their ability to be present and available and to help us feel seen.

THE COURAGE TO BE VULNERABLE

It takes courage to be vulnerable, to put yourself out there. Friendship is not a passive thing, and I can't promise you won't be hurt. I know I have been. I know what it's like to have friendships cut off because of misunderstandings, hurt feelings, or an inability to communicate. These broken relationships leave wounds of sadness and a desire to self-protect in the future.

But the risk of being known is worth the potential pain. I've tried to just say, "Thy will be done, God." And I've learned to bounce back and be open. Isolation isn't good for the soul.

> GOD PUT YOU IN THE EXACT PLACE YOU ARE FOR A REASON.

Don't wait for the "right" anything—the right city, the right house, the right moment. God put you in the exact place you are for a reason. He has already picked out your next assignment, so put yourself out there. Follow God's leading. You won't regret it.

Remember, everything has a season. Some friendships may be vibrant for a time and then go on the back burner. And that's okay. Does it mean anything's wrong with you (or the other person)? No. It's just time to see what God has next for you.

Whatever you do, breathe in the truth that God has already ordained the right friends to come alongside you in this season—and the next one.

Your Turn to Take a Breath

Write down the names of two women you admire but don't know well yet. What is it you like about them? Reach out to them and ask if they'd like to go for a walk or a cup of tea. You never know who might become a dark-alley friend!

REAL FRIENDS DO

real life together—

NO FILTER, NO MAKEUP.

CHAPTER 9

DEALING WITH PAIN

Admitting When You're Not Fine

If your friend is grieving, please, don't try to preach them out of their grief. Sit with them in it until words become necessary.

JACKIE HILL PERRY

Picture this: It's the New Orleans Saints versus the Dallas Cowboys at home in the Mercedes-Benz Superdome. Sunday Night Football. I went with no kids since it was a night game. I was decked out in black and gold, and I sat five rows up on the Saints sideline.

At the start of the game, Benjamin made his way onto the field. He spotted me in the stands and waved. It was a tradition for us to make eye contact before kickoff—something we started early in his NFL career.

He liked knowing where I was so he could see me at halftime and when he was running off the field after the game. That moment was always special for us.

All football games are physical, even at the college level. But in the NFL, the athletes are faster and stronger and know how to tackle well. This particular game was shaping up to be really rough. By halftime a few players on both teams had been hurt already, so each time Benjamin touched the ball, I was on extra high alert. Every muscle in me tensed, and I stopped breathing every down Benjamin took.

When quarterback Drew Brees threw a pass to Benjamin in the end zone, the fans leapt to their feet to see what would happen next. Benjamin caught the ball, and the crowd went wild. I cheered too—then I froze. I'd seen his catch, but as his wife, I saw something more.

While he was in the air, Benjamin was hit and his body went limp. I watched in horror as he hit the ground. A collective groan went up from the crowd as the ball rolled from his hands. He lay on the turf, motionless.

"Get up, Baby," I whispered.

I could barely breathe. In spite of the hordes of people around me, I felt alone. A thousand anxious thoughts raced through my mind. What if I lost him?

What would I do without my very best friend, the father of my kids, our family's leader, our provider? I was barely keeping it together as it was, with an infant son and four kids under five. How could I possibly do it all alone, thousands of miles from either of our families?

"Come on, Baby, get up," I whispered—or was I shouting? "Get up, please!"

BREAKABLE

It wasn't the first time somebody I loved got hurt. And it wouldn't be the last.

To make a long story short, Benjamin got up that night. Doctors determined he'd suffered a concussion. All the helmets and pads and precautions in the world can't keep men that size who are running at full speed from getting hurt once in a while. Over the course of his career, Benjamin suffered several injuries, not to mention a pretty scary case of appendicitis. Today he says he's fully recovered, although he's still pretty beat up from all his years in the NFL.

As upsetting as that moment was, we knew that a concussion was par for the course. Benjamin had more doctor visits, hospital trips, and physical therapy sessions than I can count. Our kids have also had occasional bumps, bruises, illnesses, and cuts. Through it all, I've always prided myself on keeping a level head. Somehow we always managed. I could take it in stride. And then something unexpected happened.

My own body betrayed me.

UPROOTED

Before we married, Benjamin and I planned to have four kids. That was our magic number. By the time we moved to New Orleans, we had our four—two girls and two boys. They had built-in friends. We thought our family was complete.

New Orleans was where I learned to lower my guard and put down roots, even though we knew we'd leave when Benjamin's contract was up in three years. We got involved with a great church and had amazing friends there. We experienced a new level of comfort and connection.

Maybe that's why God surprised us with Eden—our number five—in New Orleans.

It was a fruitful, beautiful season for our family. Then Benjamin signed with the Ravens. Up came those roots we'd put down. We were moving again—this time to Baltimore. As much as I'd loved New Orleans, I knew my place was with my husband and our kids, the most important people in the world to me. My people.

When we were new in Baltimore, I began thinking maybe we should try for another baby.

Now I've always liked even numbers. It might sound strange, but maybe I can explain it. With even numbers, every kid has a hand to hold, a partner for chores or homework, someone to ride roller coasters with at Disney World. You know, the important stuff!

Benjamin, however, didn't think we should have another kid. He'd grown up with lots of siblings, and our five felt like plenty to him. We talked about it and prayed about it, and still he was unmoved. Neither of us felt persuaded to change our mind.

Though I still wanted to try for another baby, I decided to keep quiet and respect Benjamin's stance. I told God, "I'll leave it in your hands." After all, God held the power to change Benjamin's mind—if that was His will.

A few months later, the Holy Spirit moved. Benjamin came up to me one day and said, "Let's do it. Let's try for another baby."

HOPEFUL

It didn't take long. Soon I felt my body signaling that I was pregnant. I'd been pregnant often enough that I just knew. Still, I didn't take a test right away. We went to England for an away game first. When I got home, I took a pregnancy test, which confirmed we were pregnant. I felt just a little off, with some morning sickness—and also full of hope.

We held off telling anyone right away. We planned to wait until the second trimester, like we had with our other five. I remember thinking that by the time we were twelve weeks in, we could send out our annual Christmas cards announcing a new Watson baby on the way.

Since we imagined this would be our last baby, Benjamin started taking pictures of my belly every week, chronicling the growth. Although we noticed the baby seemed small compared to the others, it didn't worry me at all. Every baby is different, right? Then I experienced some spotting. Not one to panic, I took it in stride. I figured we'd wait things out. No need for alarm. Besides, I hadn't found an ob-gyn in Baltimore yet. And with Benjamin in full football mode, I had my hands full at home.

Still, something told me to reach out to our midwife in Ohio. She'd delivered three of our babies, and she knew me well. I trusted her. So I told her what was going on and asked her opinion. She recommended I go ahead and find a doctor.

"If nothing else, go in and get your blood levels tested," she said. "I think it's time."

That was the first moment that I felt nervous—maybe even a little panicked. We didn't have any close friends in Baltimore yet. Who would I ask for a doctor recommendation? Then I remembered a young mom I'd met recently.

I didn't give any details. I just said, "Can I have the name of the doctor who delivered your baby?"

She gave me his name.

It was a group practice and I couldn't get the doctor she'd mentioned, so I took whoever was available. This was a decision I later came to regret. Maybe things would have been different if Benjamin could have come with me. But I didn't have a sitter, so I scheduled an appointment on Tuesday, Benjamin's only day off, so he could stay home with the kids.

I went alone.

After the doctor got a brief history and my vitals, he said, "It doesn't look to me like you're pregnant."

That's literally what he said. I didn't know whether to punch him in the face or burst out crying.

I was like, "Excuse me, sir, I know my body." As if I hadn't already carried five kids to term.

He said, "Let's just get your blood levels taken to make sure."

Wait, what? I hadn't thought this through. Where was Benjamin? I'm terrified of needles. I even had my last three babies naturally, without an epidural—that's how much I despise needles.

I was alone. And I didn't want any part of this. But what else could I do?

"I'm sorry, ma'am, but I will pass out on you," I said to the woman drawing my blood. "I just have to know: Are you really good?" I pretty much always ask that question in a lighthearted way, but this time I was spinning out.

"Oh, I'm good, baby," she said, "I've been doing this for so long . . ." She started making small talk, trying to get me to not think about that needle.

Her compassion went right to my heart, and I started crying. I told her everything. "I think I'm losing my baby," I said. I couldn't believe I was pouring my heart out to this complete stranger—God bless her!

She caught all my feelings from what had just happened with the doctor. And she was such a comfort. I'll never forget how she met me right where I was and listened with compassion and kindness.

COUCH PRAYER

The doctor called the next day with my test results. "You're pregnant," he said.

I wanted to say, *No kidding, dummy!*

He told me I needed to come in for an ultrasound.

Okay, more tests? Who has time for this? I promised that when we got back from Virginia, where Benjamin was giving a convocation address at Liberty University, I absolutely would.

Our plan was to take the whole family to Virginia since it was just a couple of hours away and it was a bye week.

But the doctor insisted I get the ultrasound that very afternoon.

Okay, fine, I thought. *I'll go.*

I remember sitting on our couch in Baltimore. My appointment was in two hours, and the kids were upstairs with Benjamin. I prayed, "God, I thought you wanted me to do this. Ultimately this baby is for you, so whatever is going to happen, prepare me for it. Help me to be strong through this."

In that moment, I instantly felt lighter in my belly, like something had been removed. It sounds strange, I know, but I just knew the baby was gone.

I began to cry. I went upstairs to tell Benjamin what

had happened. He wrapped me in a hug. He grieved with me and comforted me. He prayed with me before I went to the ultrasound later that day.

Again I went by myself. I watched the technician's face as she looked at the monitor. "I don't see anything there but the sack," she said. "There's not a baby in there."

What could I say? She was telling me what I already knew.

The technician got the doctor, and he gave the situation some official name—big words that meant nothing to me and somehow only made me feel worse. Why would I even care what he said? He'd insisted I wasn't pregnant when I knew I was, then he'd declared I was and yet now I wasn't. I felt numb. His assessment was meaningless to me. Then he said something that did matter.

"You'll still go into labor in the next week or so. It could happen anytime, so be prepared."

On top of everything else, there's this to look forward to? I thought. *I get to pack us all up for a trip where I'll be a supportive wife to Benjamin and a mom to all these people, and at some unknown place and time, my body will go into excruciating labor but there will be no baby.* It was all too absurd. I decided to leave that office and carry on. That was the extent of my ability to deal with the news he'd given me.

ILLEGALLY PARKED IN LYNCHBURG

The next day we left for Lynchburg, Virginia. At Liberty University, they really rolled out the red carpet. Benjamin did a great job, and I felt proud of and happy for him, even through the cloud of the loss.

The next day we got in the car to return to Baltimore. We'd barely left when I was hit by intense pain. We pulled over to the side of the road, and Benjamin called David Nasser, the Liberty campus chaplain. David told us how to get to the best, closest hospital. While I went in, Benjamin stayed in the Suburban with the kids. He put in a movie to keep them busy. I walked into the ER, alone. Again.

David and his family brought the kids dinner from Chick-fil-A. I will never forget the kindness they showed us when we needed it. I wouldn't have planned for something like this to happen when we were out of town, but God was so generous to provide support in unexpected ways. After all, we really didn't have community in place yet to navigate such a rocky issue in Baltimore.

I stayed in the ER for five hours. My pain subsided, and although I'd lost a lot of blood, the sac was still intact. The doctor was nervous but allowed us to drive home, considering we were so close and we had all our kids with us.

I was wheeled out of the hospital in a wheelchair to our illegally parked Suburban. Benjamin and I had to tell the kids what was going on. I don't know how much sense I was making since I was still in a haze from the medication, not to mention the emotions of it all.

The kids were so quiet. I'm sure they'd been trying to piece together all the information—overhearing strange phone calls, mom going to the doctor, a trip to the hospital.

Then, as crazy as it sounds, we drove home. We had a soccer tournament to get to. Life goes on, right?

My doctor scheduled a D&C two days later so we could make it to my daughter's soccer tournament. I drove to the final game separately so I could head to the procedure afterward. We didn't have anyone to watch the kids, so Benjamin had to stay with them. After I was done, he brought everyone in their pj's to pick me up.

After that, our life was business as usual. The kids had school and Benjamin had football and I had my hands full managing it all. We just kept moving, putting the pregnancy behind us like a bad dream. We did call our parents to let them know, but they hadn't known we were pregnant, so I don't really know how they took the news. I did know that I was hurt. I felt alone. I couldn't believe what had just happened.

SOLDIERING ON

What else could I do? My people needed me, so I put on my brave face. I taught. I sang. I did laundry. I cooked. I cleaned. I organized. I changed diapers. I read stories. I played games. I did dishes. I fell into bed exhausted every night, then woke up to do it all again.

Benjamin didn't want to try for another baby again— at least not right away. He felt like we should wait and seek God's will. I followed his lead in that, even though inside I felt a bit impatient. I don't think I was fully dealing with the loss yet. I was just powering through.

At Christmas, I got our cards printed. I remember seeing that card and thinking, *I was pregnant in this picture. This was supposed to be our announcement of the baby.* But again I just pushed through, soldiering on.

We waited a couple of months before we decided to try again. We were on the same page, both feeling like the Lord was leading us to have another child.

I got pregnant right away.

One week. Two weeks. Three weeks. Four weeks. Five weeks went by.

Then the same thing happened. This time I knew immediately what was going on. And I called a different doctor.

This time when I went in for an ultrasound, Benjamin was with me. I watched the face of the technician. *This is not good,* I thought.

She excused herself to get the doctor. He was gentle and understanding and explained, in kinder terms than the first doctor had, what was going to happen next. That was a blessing. But I already knew what to anticipate. It wasn't going to be good.

SAYING IT OUT LOUD

Two miscarriages in four months was exhausting and lonely.

In the quiet moments before sleep, one word echoed in my head: *Why?*

I didn't want to have to go to the emergency room again, so we scheduled a D&C. Benjamin stayed home with the kids while I drove to the doctor's office alone.

At the follow-up appointment, I was in the ob-gyn's waiting room, surrounded by pregnant women. I felt sadness well up inside me, threatening to pull me under. I nearly broke down into sobs right there.

Instead, I pulled out my phone and typed a few lines, then posted it to social media. Here's what I wrote:

As I sit in a crowded room of pregnant women, I wait to see the doctor 2.5 weeks after my second miscarriage in 4 months. I rest on 2 Corinthians 12:9: "But he said to me, 'My grace is sufficient for you, for my power is made perfect in weakness.'"

THE PAIN DOESN'T NECESSARILY GO AWAY; IT WILL STILL HURT. BUT GOD CAN GIVE US A NEW PERSPECTIVE.

I know that I'm not alone in this room. The sadness of losing a baby has been felt by many women who live on without uttering a word about it. They suffer in silence. Today, right now, I rejoice with women who are carrying life within their bellies and I cry with those who long for it.

My phone began to ping right away with supportive responses from friends—affirmations and prayers and reminders of God's faithfulness. The pain didn't go away; it still hurt. I just had a new perspective. That was the start of God doing something new in me and my life.

The sadness after the second miscarriage hit me doubly hard—maybe because I hadn't really grieved the first.

Benjamin kept asking, "Are you okay?"

I really wasn't. My conversations with God were all over the place. When I managed to find a moment to myself, the noise in my head was loud. All the questions echoed, taunting me. *What went wrong? Was it something I did? Something I didn't do? Did I misunderstand God's will?*

Since then I've spoken with many women who have experienced fertility issues. So many of us cry out to God, "I've been faithful. I've followed You. Why can't I have a baby?" These are tough questions, even for the faithful. It's terrible to feel like what you want is something genuinely good, and yet God allows you to walk through something so hard.

I cried a lot, and Benjamin was worried about me. Several times he said I needed to go talk to somebody. The second hospital in Baltimore offered group therapy and even a funeral service for people who had lost a baby that month. They cared for us well, offering opportunities to process our feelings. I didn't take advantage of them, though. I was in a wrestling match with God.

I remember looking at Benjamin straight in the eyes

at one point and assuring him, "You don't have to worry about me. I'm not going to turn away from God—I'm just wrestling with Him. I need some time to mourn, to grieve, to be angry."

Since we'd waited for that arbitrary twelve-week mark to tell people about the pregnancy, we didn't have anyone praying for us or rejoicing with us, and it also meant we had nobody to mourn with us when we lost the baby. The fact is, life is life—let's celebrate that as soon and as often as we can! Let's share the news with the people who love us and care for us and will pray for us. Then, heaven forbid, if something happens, they will not only celebrate with us but also mourn that life with us.

LIFE IS LIFE—
LET'S CELEBRATE
THAT AS SOON
AND AS OFTEN
AS WE CAN!

The pain of losing a child never goes away entirely. Even now I wish my babies were here. My prayer is that God can redeem that pain, allowing me to bless and encourage women who experience something similar.

DON'T SAY I DIDN'T WARN YA

Where did we get this idea that we can achieve a problem-free life? It's like we say to ourselves, *If I'm just smart enough, pretty enough, willful enough, and good enough my problems will go away.* As if we can charm, work, think, strategize, or pay our way to ease and comfort. Do you have problems? Work harder. Be smarter. Be prettier. Argue louder. The list of strategies goes on, yet problems persist.

However, Jesus assured us that troubles are a guarantee. He said, "In the world *you will have tribulation*" (John 16:33, esv, emphasis added). He didn't gloss over or soft-sell this truth. He spelled it out. But is that where he stopped? No! He said, "Take heart; I have overcome the world." Bad things will happen; it's just not the end of the story. The end has already been written, and it is good.

Francis Chan says we need to have the mindset of Christ when—not if—suffering comes. Don't be confused by it or disoriented by it. Instead, see pain as the opportunity it is: God's will at work. God isn't into giving us pain just for the sake of pain. He's into redeeming our pain. He's the God who transformed the nasty, wicked cross into a place of redemption for all of humanity. Now that's a creative act!

As our loving Father, God redeems and transforms our trials. If we don't acknowledge this reality, any infringement on "the good life" can send us into a funk. We'll feel entitled to ease and comfort, like spoiled children. Jesus said it this way: "I am sending you out like sheep among wolves" (Matthew 10:16). That's no joke, right? Wolves eat sheep, sisters! Jesus was going out of His way to say, "As My followers, you're going to experience things that are brutal at times."

BREATHE IN THE PROMISE

Yes, we will suffer. Jesus expected to suffer, and He turned it into something beautiful. He took abuse, hatred, and shame and turned it into glory, grace, and reconciliation.

Clearly, I'm not capable of anything to that measure. I don't have to be Christ, but He is in me. And through Him, my suffering can be turned into something beautiful.

Confronted with the proof of my lack of control, I have a choice:

a) kick and scream and pretend, or
b) surrender to the control of a merciful Father.

Ultimately, I know my Father's will for me is brighter and more glorious than anything I could ever design. So I'm doing my best to remember to surrender—on a daily basis.

I thank God that even in the struggle, even in the hard times, His presence is constant. His peace is right there, just a breath away. His power protects me, and His peace is beyond understanding. In all this, God is good. And He continues to pour out blessing.

BE REAL—WITH GOD, YOURSELF, AND OTHERS

Where did we learn this irrational narrative that we need to keep our "negative" emotions to ourselves? While it's probably inappropriate to unload anger, sadness, and the like on the UPS delivery person, God doesn't need us to filter with Him. He can take all our emotions, even the ones that seem embarrassing or uncomfortable to us.

So let's say hard things to Him. After all, "Nothing in all creation is hidden from God's sight" (Hebrews 4:13). In other words, He already knows how we're feeling anyway!

Instead of medicating our pain and trying to quickly move on, may we have the grace to embrace the experience we're in—not to wallow in it, but to allow us to bring it to the Lord so He can heal us. Feeling it is the only way to move into the next thing God has for us.

Looking back, I wish I'd shared my pain with others sooner. Why did I keep what I was going through to myself? I see now that keeping my pain bottled up took a lot of energy. I told myself I was holding it together when really I was imploding.

I'm learning this is not what God wants for us. God wired us to be in genuine relationship with others. Genesis 2:18 says, "It is not good for the man to be alone"—that's literally the first "not good" in Creation! In Christ, we're part of a body that wants to care for us. Our sisters and brothers can't do that if we don't tell them what's going on.

Have you ever held something in, thinking, *I don't want to be a burden*? I've said this too! Honestly, this is motivated by pride. We don't want to be seen as out of control, so we mask what we're going through.

God wants us to share our burdens. When we do, it allows us to connect in two ways:

1. Sharing our burdens creates space for others to bless us as we heal. When we give people a glimpse into our pain, we allow them to be there for us, to come alongside us. Maybe they'll do that with a shoulder to cry on or a casserole for dinner or a phone call or a gift. Think about it— giving to others feels so good. Would you deny others that gift?

2. Our particular sorrows make us experts for the next person who experiences something similar to what we've gone through.

So if you're going through something that hurts, don't hoard your hurt. Allow God to redeem it instead.

PRAISE ANYWAY

When I'm hurting, I don't always feel like opening my Bible, but I've found that the Lord meets me on the pages of His Word. Reading the Old Testament helps me see that there is a happy ending for the people of God—namely, Jesus was coming into the world through their line. They just couldn't always see it because they were in the middle of it. Reading the New Testament shows me who Jesus is and reminds me that the Holy Spirit is living inside me. What an incredible gift!

Worship music and worship services are lifelines for me when I'm going through seasons of pain and loss. "Thy Will" by Hillary Scott and the Scott Family was on replay for me in the aftermath of our miscarriages:

When I try to pray,
All I've got is hurt and these four words:
Thy will be done.

There were times when I'd be singing certain songs and I'd come to a line I simply couldn't sing along with. My breath would catch in my throat, and I'd pray, "I can usually sing this, Lord, but right now it hurts too much!" There's no reason to pretend with God. He doesn't need that. He wants us to bring our real selves. That's what genuine relationship is, after all.

I'm gonna praise Him for what has happened and what hasn't happened . . . yet! I choose to accept that God is in control, even when troubles come. I can praise the One who is always good, knowing He is pouring out blessings, even in the mess.

Little did know that wasn't the end of the story. A few months later, I was pregnant with . . . identical twin boys!

Your Turn to Take a Breath

What pain have you been trying to hide or medicate? Maybe it's time to share it—with God and a trusted friend. Go ahead and offer up thanks for what God will do in and through you because of this current struggle. Then choose someone you trust and open up to them about what you're going through.

BAD THINGS WILL HAPPEN;

IT'S JUST NOT

the end

OF THE STORY.

CHAPTER 10

AFTER THE FLOOD

Breathing Deep, Even When Your Socks Are Soaking Wet

When we fake fine, we fake our way out of authentic relationship
with God, others, and ourselves.

ESTHER FLEECE

We started off 2020 feeling good. I remember Benjamin talking about how this was going to be a big year for him—he was turning the big four-oh.

Then we learned that Kobe Bryant had been killed in a deadly plane crash, along with his daughter and seven other people. It seemed strange that someone who was so young and vibrant and had everything going for him, someone so internationally loved, could be cut down in his prime. We'd hardly wrapped our heads around that when we learned that a deadly virus was sweeping the globe—a certified pandemic. The death toll began to tick up quickly. News channels kept a running tally on their screens. As officials issued previously unheard-of "stay at home" orders, our primary concern became maintaining some degree of normalcy in our home. It all seemed so surreal.

Then George Floyd was murdered by police. This wasn't the first time a Black man was senselessly killed in police custody, and people worried that the deaths and abuse would continue. Protests began, riots broke out, and heated conversations ensued.

All of this before the year was even half finished, and we still had to make it through what was arguably the most contentious presidential election in our nation's history.

Wait. Did I mention the toilet paper shortage?

The near-constant upheaval and unrest made my head hurt. We heard the word *unprecedented* so much, it lost all real impact.

At the end of 2020, Benjamin and I realized our family needed some fresh air. After all, the nine of us had been cooped up in one house for almost ten months. I'd read that the "happiest place on earth" had just opened up to the public after months of closure, so

I set my sights on Disney. Some happiness and make-believe—that was just what we needed.

As a family, we also wanted to refocus on the meaning of Christmas. So instead of decorating and giving physical presents, we decided to mark our celebration of Jesus' birth in a new way—together, but without the usual trappings.

That trip was just what we needed. Don't get me wrong—it was a zoo, like always. Taking our seven kids anywhere is rowdy. But this trip offered us a change of scenery, plus shared adventures.

We celebrated Christmas Day as never before. Without the decorations, trees, and all the gifts, I felt more focused. At first I wondered if our kids would feel like they were missing out in some way, but as we sat in the hotel room and read Luke 2, reflecting on the Savior entering the world as a tiny, vulnerable little person, we were filled with joy.

We noted the stark contrast between our comfortable hotel room and the humble circumstances of that divine birth. On that holy night, there was no room at the inn. No room service, no ice machine, not even running water. Just a rude stable with donkeys, hay, and a stinky feed bed that the young mother used for a cradle.

The kids drank it all in, and truth be told, so did I.

The whole trip worked wonders, renewing my energy and spirit.

I returned to Boston feeling relaxed. I'm usually pretty type A when I get home from a trip, ready to attack the laundry and my to-do list. This time I was floating on cloud nine. As we got out of the van, I thought, *I'm gonna give myself a break—maybe order pizza and enjoy this vacation a little longer.*

Walking in, I heard a faint sound—a little *beep, beep.* Could we have left the freezer open this whole time? I went to the kitchen and checked. Nope, the freezer was closed. Was it the dishwasher? No, not the dishwasher, either. Where was the sound coming from? I sent the big kids upstairs to get into their pajamas with the promise of a shared movie, then put the twins down for bed.

When I got downstairs, I realized Benjamin had disappeared. Soon I heard him say, "Oh no."

I found him on the stairs leading to the finished basement.

"What happened?" I stood beside him and looked at his face. He seemed to be in shock. Then I noticed my socks were soaking wet—the carpet was saturated.

Long story short, the sump pump had quit working and our basement flooded. By this point, all the water had receded, but there had been a lot of it. We could tell because Benjamin's heavy massage table had floated about twenty feet across the room. All our furniture, the toys, the boxes of photographs, mementos, and baby things—all drenched.

Benjamin was visibly upset. "How could I have let this happen?" he asked.

I hugged him. "It's not your fault, Babe," I said. "It's gonna be okay."

In Florida we'd been talking about priorities—about how Jesus is what matters, not the stuff the world tells us Christmas is about. I'd even quoted this Scripture: "Do not store up for yourselves treasures on earth, where moth and rust consume and where thieves break in and steal" (Matthew 6:19, NRSV).

Now it was time to walk out that truth.

When we went upstairs, our kids saw our faces and immediately asked, "What's wrong?"

We told them what had happened and that we didn't know if anything could be salvaged.

When Benjamin sweetly apologized, they said, "Daddy, it's not your fault." They hugged him—and me too.

You know what they said next? "Now can we watch a movie together?"

Over the next few weeks we had to throw out a lot of things. As the insurance adjusters and construction workers came and went, it was a little unnerving for all of us. But the overarching feeling was, *This is a little sad and a little hard, but ultimately, it's all okay.*

GOOD THING I'M NOT IN CHARGE

The flood in our basement surprised me. It didn't surprise God. He didn't cause it, yet in His sovereignty, He knew it was coming and used it for His good—to mature us and draw us closer to Him.

In my mind, life would have been so much nicer if we had avoided that whole issue. I'd go back in time and fix that sump pump prior to our Disney trip and save us the trouble. But if I'd done that, who knows what I would have missed out on? It's a good thing God is in charge and not me!

> IT'S A GOOD THING GOD IS IN CHARGE AND NOT ME!

I don't know about you, but I can be so stubborn. I sing, "Take me deeper than my feet could ever wander," but when He stretches me, do I thank Him? I can quote James about rejoicing in perseverance, yet when adversity comes, do I rejoice? Easier said than done.

So I pray, "Lord, I believe; help my unbelief!" (Mark 9:24).

Those rising waters weren't something I asked for, and they weren't something I'd wish on anyone. But there were blessings for me there—lessons way more valuable than the stuff we lost.

After any storm or trial, we'll see His blessings . . . if we have eyes to see. The strongest rains and winds won't wash His blessings away.

DETACHMENT

Our New Orleans friends were familiar with loss. We had close friends who lost everything in Hurricane Katrina—their entire homes had been destroyed. Of course, that was long before we lived there.

I remember watching coverage about Hurricane Katrina on the news. It was our first year of marriage, when we were living in Boston. I remember feeling sympathy and wishing I could help. This was trauma on a grand scale—it marked everyone who lived there permanently. Think of it: a lifetime of memories, wiped out in a day.

When our little basement flooded, I realized it was nothing compared to a loss of that magnitude. As I thought of our friends in New Orleans, I no longer felt just sympathy; I felt empathy—and so much respect.

There's a beautiful resilience that can come from

dealing with loss. As so many of our NOLA friends say, "Loss teaches you not to hold things too close." I like that.

As a mother and a wife, I spend a lot of time making sure my family has what they need. I'm the designated shopper and chooser. Our basement incident etched on my heart that I'm just the steward of these things—they were never mine to begin with. Everything I have is God's. I want to hold everything with open hands.

Some irreplaceable things in the basement couldn't be saved, like photos and mementos from when the children were babies. It made me sad to lose those things forever. As I went through the mementos, I celebrated the good they represented and thanked God for the living, breathing people they pointed me to.

When it came to replaceable things that had to be thrown out, my priorities were clearer than ever. Did we really need this toy or game? Or could the time and money be better spent creating memories—something that can't be taken away?

It's okay to have things. What's not okay is for things to have you. As human beings, we have a materialistic bent—we want to possess and own. There's nothing

THERE'S A BEAUTIFUL RESILIENCE THAT CAN COME FROM DEALING WITH LOSS.

wrong with having nice things. I just want to guard my heart and make sure things aren't owning me. That's one way the flood offered a reality check for me. It forced me to evaluate how much we're invested in our stuff.

ACCEPTING A HELPING HAND

My impulse was to handle our ruined basement as quietly and quickly as possible. My goal was to get back to normal ASAP, with as little drama as possible. I didn't want anyone outside our family to know. I'm not sure why, exactly—maybe I thought it would show weakness or something, not unlike Benjamin's reaction when he felt like it was his fault.

When I'm dealing with stress, I have a tendency to minimize whatever I'm going through. My brain tells me, *It isn't a big deal. Plenty of people are dealing with so much worse. I just need to suck it up.*

Benjamin doesn't suffer from this problem. He told everyone he talked to about our flooded basement. And you know what? Lots of people wanted to help! One friend offered fans to dry out the basement. Other people offered names of contractors who'd helped them with similar problems. Once the cat was out of the bag, I began to talk about it too. To my surprise, people didn't judge us; they rallied around us with support.

When we risk being vulnerable and sharing our story, it creates a bond of understanding that connects us with other people. We pray differently for other people when we know what they're going through. Our connections run deeper and make our prayers that much more specific and fervent.

The enemy would do everything in his power to make sure we don't share our struggles. He wants to divide us, and one of his most common strategies is to isolate us. If we go it alone, we're more vulnerable to his lies. God wants more for us. That's why we're part of a body—a community of people who can help us through the challenges we face.

It takes courage to share the not-so-pretty parts of our lives—the failures, the trials, the out-of-control things. But experience is teaching me that it's worth the risk.

FOUND IN THE RUBBLE

One of the unexpected joys of this whole experience was how our kids reacted when we told them what happened. They were more concerned about us and spending time together than in the stuff they'd lost. This made my momma heart so happy. It felt like a wink from God, saying, *See what happens when you lead them as I've called you to do?*

Fast-forward to several weeks later, when the basement was put back together and the kids could go down and play. All we'd been able to salvage was a box of blocks, a bag of Legos, a wooden table, and two trucks. That's it. Do you know what my kids did? They walked past the small pile of toys and started a game of tag. They loved all the open space!

My youngest girl came over to me and asked, "Mommy, is this all that was saved from the flood?"

"Yes, Baby, that's it!"

She looked around and said, "At least Levi and Asher have their trucks!"

I nodded and smiled as she ran off to join her siblings in their game of tag.

THE LONG VIEW

The next time my socks are soaking wet, so to speak, I'll remember that keeping my eyes downcast does little good. I want to lift my eyes and try to see the long view. *What,* I'll ask myself, *is God saying in this moment?*

One surefire way to train our minds to see the long view is to consistently stay in the Word. This year I committed to reading the Bible front to back. I feel myself getting impatient for the "good part"—the New Testament, when Jesus shows up on the scene. But what's been inspiring as I read the Old Testament is seeing how many hardships the people of God suffered through. I mean, these were His chosen ones, and they endured so much.

As I read all this with the benefit of hindsight, I want to go back in time and say, "You guys, it's going to be worth it!" I'm living with the blessing of being on the other side. I know the happy ending of their story—and our story too. It all leads up to the coming of God's Son, the forgiveness of sin, the gift of the Holy Spirit, and the promise of Christ's return.

When I think about my life and how I feel at any given moment, it can be hard because so many things are hidden. I don't know when a particular trial will be over or when things will go back to "normal"— whatever that is. Because of that, it can feel like I'm moving through thick mud.

Reading God's Word helps me lean into His goodness as I read about His faithfulness throughout the generations. When we face our storms, we don't have to just endure them; we can learn something through them. What if He is, even now, doing a new thing? As the Lord says in Isaiah 43:19, "See, I am doing a new thing!" To that, I say, "Amen!"

When you face a difficult situation, do you tend to share about it or keep it to yourself? Have you ever shared a private pain with someone and unexpectedly uncovered a positive upside? What did that experience teach you?

AFTER ANY STORM OR TRIAL, WE'LL

see His blessings...

IF WE HAVE EYES TO SEE.

CHAPTER 11

YOU DO YOU, BOO

On Unique Giftings

Great people do not do great things; God does great things
through surrendered people.

JENNIE ALLEN

I enjoy food.

Correction. I. LOVE. FOOD.

I'm the designated reservations maker for date nights with my husband. As soon as we decide on a date and put it on our calendar, I go into full-on preparation mode. I pore over menus, read reviews, and scroll through pictures taken by my fellow foodies. I book the reservations (always early!) and daydream about what

I'll order. By the time we're seated, I usually know more about the place than our server!

Benjamin, on the other hand, doesn't care much about food. He's not opposed to eating a nice meal, but he'd just as soon eat tuna fish right out of the can. Many times I've caught him eating leftover spaghetti and meatballs over the kitchen sink—cold!—to avoid the cleanup involved with warming the meal.

That's not how I roll. My passion for food extends to the way I cook for and feed my family. Nothing pleases me more than creating a meal that looks and tastes amazing for the people I love most. When my family is seated around the table and they're excited to eat what I've cooked, I'm in my happy place. It may sound old-fashioned to some, but I like to cook my family breakfast. My kids' first words to me in the morning are often, "Will you make your biscuits today?" That's a piece of the legacy I want to leave my children: that their momma cooked.

If it was up to Benjamin, our kids would eat cereal. We're different that way—and that's okay. Different is good. I used to try to persuade him to enjoy food and cooking as much as I do. After a while I realized that it's my thing, not his. He can keep his documentaries and war movies. I'll be in the kitchen, whipping up something tasty.

Over the years, I've learned that one of the ingredients to a successful marriage (and any relationship, for that matter) is the ability to appreciate each other's different gifts and preferences without trying to change them. The sooner we can figure that out, the more we'll be able to appreciate each other—and allow our gifts to work together for the Kingdom.

TWIN LESSONS

My twins teach me every day that no two people on this planet are exactly alike. Though Asher and Levi have nearly identical genetic makeups, and though they're growing up in the same environment, eating the same foods, and experiencing the same daily routines, they have such different personalities. They have their own God-given talents, strengths, and perspectives.

GOD IS ENDLESSLY CREATIVE, ISN'T HE?

God is endlessly creative, isn't He? What fires each of us up is no accident. Our passions are unique. Even our weaknesses are unique. Think about that for a minute: God has entrusted each of us with specific treasures and talents. It's our job to put them to use for Kingdom purposes.

Check out what the Word has to say about this:

In this way we are like the various parts of a human body. Each part gets its meaning from the body as a whole, not the other way around. The body we're talking about is Christ's body of chosen people. Each of us finds our meaning and function as a part of his body. But as a chopped-off finger or cut-off toe we wouldn't amount to much, would we? So since we find ourselves fashioned into all these excellently formed and marvelously functioning parts in Christ's body, let's just go ahead and be what we were made to be, without enviously or pridefully comparing ourselves with each other, or trying to be something we aren't.

ROMANS 12:4-5, MSG

Do you catch that? In the body, every part is vital. Have you ever been slicing vegetables and cut your own flesh? Ugh! Not only is it painful, but you end up working around a bandaged finger. Awkward! Even with nine perfectly good, working fingers, it's hard accomplishing what you can with ten.

You are a part of the body of Christ, and the whole

body is needed. The body doesn't need you to be someone else. No one part is more valuable than another. The body needs you, exactly as you are.

THOU SHALL NOT HAVE FOMO

The images other people post on social media can be pretty alluring. Now and then I'll see an Instagram post and think, *No spit-up stains on her shirt. Must be nice!*

And yet this person is my friend—someone I know. There's more to her story than this lovely, well-lit picture, just like there's more to mine. Her smile is hard-won—she's recently learned her mom's cancer is in remission, her friends hurt her feelings when they left her out of a recent gathering, or her child is having a tantrum off-screen. We're all going through something. And if we're not going through it right now, we're catching our breath from the last thing we went through.

So please, sister, don't poop on your life by comparing it to someone else's IG highlights. You may admire where someone is now, but there's no telling what she had to go through to get there. Remember, none of us get out of life without pain and suffering (see John 16:33).

When I feel wistful for a stress-free life, I thank God for putting me exactly where I am in this exact moment, even if I'm not loving how my pants are fitting or if my house isn't decorated like something from HGTV. I couldn't live someone else's life—and I wouldn't want to. By God's grace, I aim to make the most of the one I've got.

DO YOUR JOB

In our family, we have a saying: "Do your job." It's a saying worth unpacking here.

Benjamin has a Super Bowl ring to testify to his prowess on the football field. But when the time comes for kicking a field goal, I don't want to see Benjamin running onto the field. It's not his job. It's not what he's been trained for. His position is tight end—he blocks and catches passes. When the team needs a field goal, they send in the kicker, not the tight end.

The same goes for you and me. We need to do our job.

What is your job? It's what you've committed yourself to. It's the people you've committed to doing life with. It's living out your gifts for the Kingdom.

Each of us has been granted special giftings. God has given you a gift that's missing from the body of Christ until you use it.

Over the years I've wished many times we didn't have to move so much for my husband's job. For much of my adult life, I've been the new girl who got lots of disbelieving looks for how many kids we have. As a result, I've often felt like an outsider.

What's been so interesting is how God's used that "odd mom out" status to draw me to serve other moms. When I hear from moms who feel isolated and over-whelmed, I instantly feel like, "Me, too!" My particular experiences give me an instant connection and a sense of empathy I might not have otherwise.

The difficult things we walk through can make us feel more alive, more connected, and more aligned with God's work in the world.

MOM LIFE

As moms, we devote a lot of time, money, and energy to raising our children. It helps when we remember they're not really ours—they're on loan from God. They'll be with us for about eighteen years, and then, God willing, they'll go out into the world and do amazing things. I smile when I think of the day when they

- find something they love and they're good at
- discover they're not afraid to go where God tells them to go
- find ways to serve God and His children

- find a spouse who will honor and love them, if they choose to marry, and work together for the Kingdom of God even as they chase separate dreams

Though I never in my wildest dreams would have thought I'd be a mom to seven, God works through that role in powerful ways. He uses my gifts and passions—from my love for food to my natural curiosity to my management skills to my teaching background—to help me fulfill my calling. He has expanded my ministry beyond my family to serve other moms at MomLifeToday. I also get to share my experience of mom life in our podcast, *Why or Why Not with the Watsons.*

Your version of the mom life may look different from mine—and that's how it should be! The important thing is to use the gifts God has given you to serve the people God has given you. You just may be surprised by what He does! For my part, I continue to be surprised by how God multiplies what I offer Him. The child who gave Jesus his loaves and fish is my role model!

ON A MISSION

If you want to be more intentional about using your gifts for the Kingdom, I highly recommend coming up with a mission statement. Such a statement can help you direct your precious resources of time, money, and energy into purposes you want to invest in long term.

In our family, we chose a Bible verse for our mission statement:

> He has shown you, O mortal, what is good.
> And what does the LORD require of you?
> To act justly and to love mercy
> and to walk humbly with your God.
> MICAH 6:8

It's so simple, right? Do justice. Love mercy. Walk humbly. In succinct language, this verse points our family toward values that aren't just worthy ideals but God-given commands.

This verse guides our purpose as a family. We've committed it to memory, and we have it hanging in a prominent place in our home. It helps us to say an emphatic yes to some things and no to others—with no shame or regret.

YOU DO YOU, BOO

What makes you smile? What is *your* thing? What is it you want your people to remember about their time with you? Figure out what gets you excited. What's going to be your legacy for the Kingdom?

Sister, the person you are is beautiful. Own your identity. Nurture it. Dig in and resolve to be more of who God has made you to be. Others may not share enthusiasm for the same things, but that's okay. God's economy has room for all the gifts, and He will use what you bring Him for His glory. It's up to you to express it. Watch and see!

Your Turn to Take a Breath

Sometimes it's our quirks that point us to our legacy. For instance, my obsession with food has become a way for me to nurture my family. What quirks do you have that you can offer God for Kingdom purposes? Take a moment to offer a couple of specific things about you to God, and ask Him to show you how they fit into the body.

Our children

ARE NOT REALLY OURS—

THEY'RE ON LOAN FROM GOD.

CHAPTER 12

MY HEART'S DESIRE

The Gospel from My Point of View

Until this Gospel seems too good to be true,
you probably have not heard it!

R. T. KENDALL

While sorting through the day's mail, I discover a slick catalog from a fancy home goods store. The pages are filled with pictures of gorgeous bakeware pans, stainless steel ice cream makers, and blenders powerful enough to pull a trailer. While I don't *need* any of those things, I daydream about what it would be like to play with all these foodie toys in my future kitchen.

Then the outdoor living section catches my eye—all

that greenery appeals to me after so many snowy days in Boston. I smile, imagining grilling outdoors again. Wait, what's this? Custom brass plates for a mailbox featuring your family's name and street address? I imagine seeing *Watson* on such a plate. We've never had a permanent address before. Suddenly I'm envious of non-renters. We're still years away from our forever home, but that doesn't stop me from dreaming. While I'm at it, I want a little stamper with our address for our outgoing envelopes.

THE BIG ASK

We all want things, right? We wish for better clothes, a nicer car, a suitcase with working wheels. We think, *My life will be better when I get what I want, right?* We tell ourselves we'll be better off when our desires are fulfilled.

It doesn't have to be something from a catalog. We wish to be taller, lose the baby weight, or figure out a cure for headaches. We want to be less shy or less talkative. We hope to be more of something or less of something else.

Or maybe it's relational—we wish to be married or divorced; we wish we had kids (or different kids); we wish for a new friend group. We wish others would change or take us seriously or ask for our forgiveness or give us the respect we deserve. We wish for more time.

Longings are not bad—they're part of being human. The truth is, all our longings point to a deeper, truer desire: the desire to be known and truly loved.

Like you, I wear a lot of different hats: wife, mom, editor, podcaster, Bible study teacher, cook, lover, fighter, teacher, griever, overcomer. Each of these roles requires time and energy, and I struggle sometimes to know which role takes precedence. For instance: when my husband needs something and I'm on a Zoom call trying to be a good businessperson. Or when I'm trying to engage my child in conversation while my phone is blowing up with messages from my Bible study group.

> I CAN ONLY FIND PEACE— AND KNOW MY NEXT STEPS—WHEN I LISTEN FOR MY FATHER'S VOICE.

Whatever I'm doing at any given moment, I can only find peace—and know my next steps—when I listen for my Father's voice.

LISTENING FOR YOUR FATHER'S VOICE
I'll never forget the time our family was visiting the New Orleans Zoo when our four kids were four and under. We'd spent the morning walking the park, checking

out the animals and chatting with another family who had come along. At last we arrived at the kids' favorite exhibit. It wasn't even an animal—it was a fantastic, enormous tree the children could play on and pretend they, too, lived in the wild.

Naomi wasn't yet four years old, but she was excited to do whatever the big kids were doing. She was determined to conquer this marvelous tree, which to her was as big and inviting as the wide world. She boldly began climbing, and every so often I'd check on her progress. She was doing great . . . until she looked down and saw how high she was.

Suddenly she froze. She couldn't go back the way she'd come, and she couldn't go up any farther. Kids were coming behind her, but she was too frightened to move another inch. She wouldn't budge. Kids were getting impatient, urging her to move.

I could see that Naomi needed help, but she was too high for me to reach. I didn't want my girl to fall. So I took a deep breath and in my calmest voice said, "Naomi, you gotta take another step. You can do it."

I verbally guided her across the branch, coaxing her to a place where she could safely jump down. It took what felt like an eternity. I kept my voice steady as she inched forward. "You've got this, girl. I'm right here."

At last she was within my reach. I plucked her down and hugged her tight. Then she scampered off to run and play some more.

My friend had been watching the whole time. As I joined her on the bench, I saw that tears were streaming down her face. "Why are you crying?" I asked.

"There was so much noise—twenty other kids hollering around her," my friend said. "Yet for Naomi, the only voice she heard was yours. And it made all the difference."

That's exactly what God does for us. Jesus said, "His sheep follow him because they know his voice" (John 10:4). When we're listening for Him, the noise all around us fades.

THIS WAY, GUYS!

Naomi's path that day wasn't intended for all the children there. She needed specific guidance, just for her. The other kids had different assignments, different paths to take. The same goes for you and me. The Father directs us individually, if we let Him. He invites us into an intimate conversation with Him.

What I want you to hear is this: as much as we can learn from one another, the most important thing we can do is listen for God's voice and follow it. You'll hear it in Scripture, and you'll hear it in your interactions with the Holy Spirit. The more you listen to Him, the more your desires will be aligned with His desires. And that's when God will truly grant you the desires of your heart, because they will be His desires for you.

Our relationship with God—the Creator of the universe, the Giver of life, the Light of the world—is made possible only by the sacrifice of Jesus Christ. That goodness is way too glorious to keep to ourselves! His love and compassion and mercy are for everyone, and He invites all people into intimate relationship with Him. That invitation is to abundant, eternal life. And He calls you and me to share that news with the world.

After Jesus' resurrection, before He returned to heaven, He gave His followers one final assignment, often called the Great Commission. The charge is for us, too:

> Then the eleven disciples went to Galilee, to
> the mountain where Jesus had told them to
> go. When they saw him, they worshiped him;
> but some doubted. Then Jesus came to them
> and said, "All authority in heaven and on
> earth has been given to me. Therefore go and
> make disciples of all nations, baptizing them

in the name of the Father and of the Son and
of the Holy Spirit, and teaching them to obey
everything I have commanded you. And surely I
am with you always, to the very end of the age."
MATTHEW 28:16-20

This feels like a rather daunting calling to me. When
I feel pressure to share about what Jesus has done, I
hear a voice inside saying, *I know you're scared, Kirsten.
I know it feels like you can't, but you can.* The Holy Spirit
is pointing out the next step the whole time. My part
is to listen, to really hear that guiding voice. The Holy
Spirit directs; it's on me to take the next step.

Like Naomi on that huge tree, I don't know where
the next step will lead. But I trust the voice leading me.

SHINE ON

I grew up in a Catholic home. We were always in church
and were active members in Sunday school. I grew up
knowing God and knowing the gospel—and knowing
that I was God's child. I felt special, the daughter of
royalty. I didn't know my Father very well, but I figured
that was the price of being royalty.

When I was in seventh grade, a teacher shared with
me how the gospel invites us into a relationship with

the almighty God. For the first time, I understood that an invitation to a relationship requires a yes or no response. She shared how my response would help me know where I would be spending eternity. And by knowing God and accepting Him as my Lord and Savior, I wouldn't have to rely on my good works to get me into heaven.

My relationship with Jesus took root then and there, because I said yes! I truly felt like a new person. Ever since I accepted that invitation, I live "by faith in [Jesus], who loved me and gave himself for me" (Galatians 2:20).

That invitation isn't just for me—it's for you, too. It's for everyone!

Perhaps as you read this, you are in the middle of something so tough you hardly have the strength to face another day. You feel stuck. Every breath feels like an effort because of the pain and anxiety you're feeling. If that's you, try this: whisper the name of Jesus. He's right there. This little act of faith sounds small, but it's really huge.

Even when you're not pursuing God, He's pursuing you. Your loving Father sees you, knows you, and loves you. He longs to bless you—all you need to do is call on Him.

This life-giving news, this oxygen, is too good to keep to ourselves. When you've got something this good, you have to share it!

The presence of Christ lights a candle in our hearts. So as you shine with His light, I expect soon you'll be hearing from the people around you. Your light will attract their curiosity, and they'll ask, "How do you do it?"

Share that fresh air, will you? I know you will!

THE GOOD NEWS IS TOO GOOD TO KEEP TO OURSELVES.

Your Turn to Take a Breath

It still blows my mind when I think about the fact that in Christ, I am fully forgiven, fully known, and fully accepted by God. Close your eyes and breathe in this fact. Feel the power of it in your body, all the way down to your toes. Experience that joy—and let it radiate from you!

EVEN WHEN YOU'RE NOT

pursuing God,

HE'S PURSUING YOU.

ACKNOWLEDGMENTS

I want to thank my dark-alley friends for helping me breathe through the process of creating this book. CD, TD, AB, AH, WL, GS, and LT—I love you all! You have brought so much to my life, and I will be forever grateful for the shared laughter and tears, prayers, inside jokes, honesty, respectful disagreements, and growth.

Creating a book is a team effort, and it's been a pleasure to work alongside a truly world-class publishing team. Thank you, Rachelle Gardner, Stephanie Rische, Jan Long Harris, Sarah Atkinson, Christina Garrison, Amy Headington, Julie Chen, Debbie King, Cassidy Gage, Amanda Woods, Nate Rische, and Megan Alexander. I am forever grateful.

NOTES

CHAPTER 4: WAGS

1. Clay Routledge, "The Surprising Power of Nostalgia at Work," *Harvard Business Review*, April 26, 2021, https://hbr.org/2021/04/the-surprising -power-of-nostalgia-at-work.

CHAPTER 7: PRAYER

1. Jon Michail, "Strong Nonverbal Skills Matter Now More than Ever in This 'New Normal,'" *Forbes*, August 24, 2020, https://www.forbes .com/sites/forbescoachescouncil/2020/08/24/strong-nonverbal-skills -matter-now-more-than-ever-in-this-new-normal/?sh=4373d6b55c61.
2. Mother Teresa, *A Simple Path* (New York: Ballantine Books, 1995), 7–8.